The Healthy Soup Cleanse Recipe Book

200+ Easy Souping Recipes from Bone Broth to Vegetable Soup!

Britt Brandon, CFNS, CPT

Avon, Massachusetts

Published by
Adams Media, a division of F+W Media, Inc.
57 Littlefield Street, Avon, MA 02322. U.S.A.
www.adamsmedia.com

Contains material adapted from *The Everything® DASH Diet Cookbook* by Christy Ellingsworth and Murdoc Khaleghi, MD, copyright © 2012 by F+W Media, Inc., ISBN 10: 1-4405-4353-4, ISBN 13: 978-1-4405-4353-1.

ISBN 10: 1-4405-9325-6
ISBN 13: 978-1-4405-9325-3
eISBN 10: 1-4405-9326-4
eISBN 13: 978-1-4405-9326-0

Printed in the United States of America.

10 9 8 7 6 5 4 3 2 1

Library of Congress Cataloging-in-Publication Data
Brandon, Britt, author.
  The healthy soup cleanse recipe book / Britt Brandon, CFNS, CPT.
    pages cm
  Includes index.
  ISBN 978-1-4405-9325-3 (pb) – ISBN 1-4405-9325-6 (pb) – ISBN 978-1-4405-9326-0 (ebook) – ISBN 1-4405-9326-4 (ebook)
  1. Soups. 2. Detoxification (Health) I. Title.
  TX757.B667 2016
  641.81'3–dc23
                    2015030433

33614056477473

The information in this book should not be used for diagnosing or treating any health problem. Not all diet and exercise plans suit everyone. You should always consult a trained medical professional before starting a diet, taking any form of medication, or embarking on any fitness or weight-training program. The author and publisher disclaim any liability arising directly or indirectly from the use of this book.

Always follow safety and commonsense cooking protocol while using kitchen utensils, operating ovens and stoves, and handling uncooked food. If children are assisting in the preparation of any recipe, they should always be supervised by an adult.

Many of the designations used by manufacturers and sellers to distinguish their products are claimed as trademarks. Where those designations appear in this book and F+W Media, Inc. was aware of a trademark claim, the designations have been printed with initial capital letters.

Cover design by Frank Rivera.
Cover photography by Erin Dawson.

This book is available at quantity discounts for bulk purchases.
For information, please call 1-800-289-0963.

CONTENTS

Chapter 8: Healthy Gut Soups 137

Chapter 9: Skin-Nourishing Soups 155

Introduction

Do you want to start your day off right with a sweet mixture of apples and cinnamon? Boost your immunity with the delicious combination of honey, ginger, and turmeric? Refresh yourself with a cool dose of avocado, cucumber, and melon?

Here in *The Healthy Soup Cleanse Recipe Book*, you'll find more than 200 delicious, detoxifying, cleansing soups that do all this and more! Whether you want to cleanse your body and mind, cure ailments and disease, restore your body to optimal health, lose weight or improve your digestive system, or would like to improve your overall health and quality of life, you'll find recipes in this book that will fit your needs. And with chapters that focus on dessert soups, bone broths, and soups specifically of the green variety, this soup-cleansing recipe book has it all! And the best part of this book (aside from sipping super soup servings every three hours and never being hungry!) is the versatility and variety of delicious and nutritious recipes that pack nutrient-dense fruits, vegetables, and additions into each of your five daily meals and snacks!

Through a daily diet of five soups consumed every three hours enjoyed in any amount you choose, your soup cleanse will ensure your body has adequate nutrition at its disposal day and night. Without hunger or feelings of starvation or restriction, each soup will keep you feeling full, focused, and energized as you embark on a total health transformation. With vibrant vegetables and delectable fruits, combined with creamy nut milks and yogurts, along with nutrient-boosting additions like nuts and seeds, these delectable recipes help keep your soup cleanse packed with easy-to-make varieties and vibrant options that you can consume at any time of the day, keeping your soup cleanse new and exciting, and nutritious and delicious! Congratulations to you for choosing *The Healthy Soup Cleanse Recipe Book* as your path to better health and a better life!

PART 1

What Is Souping?

Welcome to the wonderful world of soup cleansing! Whether your goal is to lose weight, increase energy, improve immunity, or target a specific health issue like gut health or the appearance of your skin, soup cleansing can restore the health of your body's cells and systems and rejuvenate your brain and body all while letting you enjoy delicious and nutritious soups that are packed with flavorful whole foods like vibrant vegetables, sweet fruits, and other tasty additions like yogurt, kefir, seeds, and nuts. By enjoying filling servings of your favorite soups every three hours, you deliver a variety of vitamins, minerals, and powerful phytochemicals to your brain and body, which help rid the body of toxins and replenish the stores of the essential nutrients that not only allow your body to function but to thrive! So now you know what a soup cleanse is, but how does it work? What do you have to do to be successful? What materials do you need to have on hand? Read on and get ready to heal your body and start living a life filled with energy, stamina, and a brain and body that work as designed!

CHAPTER 1

Soup Cleanse Basics

Souping is the shortened term for "soup cleansing," refer-ring to the process of relying on only soups (vibrant, deli-cious, and nutritious soups packed with sweet and savory combinations of fruits, vegetables, and additions) for your breakfasts, lunches, dinners, and snacks in an effort to achieve a health goal such as weight loss, increased energy, detox, or improved immunity. Souping stands out from other cleansing processes because this cleanse focuses on providing the body with consistent nourishment of only the healthiest, cleanest whole foods. Souping is taking the world by storm, helping people around the world live healthier, happier lives ... deliciously!

Before you start souping, cleansing your body with soups packed with natural nutrients, it is important that you take a look at why you should use a soup cleanse, how to successfully and safely try a soup cleanse, and how to stock your home with the items you need to be successful. Why? Knowing the many benefits that can result from cleansing—such as improved immunity, healthy (and easily maintained) weight loss, increased energy, reduced mental "fogginess," and reduced inflammation that can cause aches, pains, illness, and disease—can help you make the decision to experience the life-improving changes that can result from using simple, easy-to-follow cleanses on a regular basis (at least twice a year). With the information and guidance found within *The Healthy Soup Cleanse Recipe Book*, it's never been easier for you to create the perfect cleanse for your body and your schedule. Whether you choose to design a cleanse that lasts for one, three, five days, or more, you can learn how to tailor your souping with the precise benefits you seek with simplicity. Using this book, its information, and all of the plentiful delicious and nutritious recipes included, you can detoxify, rejuvenate, re-energize, and replenish your brain and body without feelings of deprivation and starvation that many normally associate with a cleanse. So prepare to put some pep in your step, have more energy during the day, experience a more rejuvenating sleep at night, and feel better than ever as you deliver optimal nutrients your body and brain need to not just function but to thrive!

How to Soup Cleanse

Hippocrates, one of the most influential people in medicine and considered the father of Western medicine, once said, "Let food be thy medicine and medicine be thy food." He believed in the power of natural foods for healing purposes that ranged from prevention and treatment to the maintenance of optimal health. Hippocrates's phrase perfectly encompasses the goals and benefits of the soup cleanse: nutrition being put to good use in the pursuit of a healthier life. With a focus on maximized nutrition, physicians thousands of years ago were able to prevent and cure ailments while ensuring total wellness, and it is that same premise on which the soup cleanse is based today, with the same goals to deliver the same benefits!

While souping may seem to have taken the health world by storm in the same way many fad diets of the past have, with celebrities, famous physicians, and countless health centers around the world adopting and promoting it as the most effective process to achieve everything from weight loss and detox to the management of illness and disease and improvement of overall health, the soup-cleansing process is anything but a new fad. With a long history of success that supports its use, the premise and routine of soup cleansing is to provide consistent nutrition that fuels the body while detoxifying and delivering maximum benefits to the body and brain. By focusing on consistent meals and snacks throughout the day designed to deliver optimal nutrition, not only does the soup cleanse keep you satisfied, but it keeps you energized and focused, helping to maintain physical and mental health and stability throughout the process. Supplying the body with delicious combinations of fruits, vegetables, and healthy additions, the soups that can be included in the soup cleanse are not only tailored to your tastes but combine nutrient-dense varieties of natural foods that add a wide array of vitamins, minerals, phytochemicals, and antioxidants.

Detoxification diets have been used throughout history as readily as prescriptions for purifying the body, so cleanses are nothing new to the world of health. These day-, week-, or month-long ventures to purge, purify, and replenish the body date back centuries. With a documented history of cleansing, the practice of purifying the body for health improvement, prevention, and even spiritual purification is a worldwide practice that is growing in popularity today. The goals of cleansing still focus on detoxification, improved system functioning, and weight loss, with the ideal result being an optimized state of health in which everything from breathing and digestion to thought processes and energy levels are improved. Through the sipping of soup, greater health can be achieved simply, and with added benefits galore!

The Benefits of Souping

In the past few decades, the Standard American Diet (appropriately termed "SAD") has changed its focus from whole, natural foods like fruits, vegetables, whole grains, and lean meats to instead include a barrage of large portions, fat-packed fast food, processed meals, and chemical-laden drink options that have led to an alarming increase in systemic conditions and diseases like allergies, obesity, and diabetes. Fortunately, the soup cleanse can turn this trend around and make sure you are happy, healthy, and satisfied—nutritionally, emotionally, and otherwise. When you realize the benefits of this detoxifying cleansing, it's easy to understand why millions of people have chosen to opt for this age-old process of natural detoxification, and why multiple cleansing centers around the world have opted for a soup-cleanse-focused diet for their detoxification and purification programs.

The overwhelming amounts of sugar, sodium, preservatives, toxins, and carcinogens found in processed food wreak havoc on the body as they pass through the digestive system and are swiftly delivered throughout the bloodstream to each and every cell and system in the body. Then, since every system in the body is tasked with the tedious processing of these toxins rather than on the processing of essential nutrients, the systems aren't able to process, store, and utilize nutrients for optimal health, growth, and performance as they're designed to do, leading to vulnerability to illness and disease and various system malfunctions.

Fortunately, with the soup cleanse, the body is only provided with nutrient-dense, toxin-free meals and is able to focus on clean sources of nutrition. When you eat the soups found in Part 2, the body is able to successfully deliver the essential vitamins, minerals, antioxidants, and phytonutrients that help restore, revive, and replenish the cells and systems throughout the body, and prepare the entire body for a return to optimal health. In addition to delivering toxin-free meals and snacks to your body, specific ingredients like garlic, ginger, turmeric, cumin, cinnamon, apple cider vinegar, probiotics, and many more all help to cleanse the body of existing toxins.

Let's take a look at the benefits of this easy and delicious trend.

Soups Are Easy to Prepare

Creating a nutrition-based meal plan can be a daunting task, but the soup cleanse recipes found in Part 2 take the guesswork out of meal preparation. In as little as an hour, you can create a wide variety of soups that you can store and enjoy throughout your soup cleanse, making the process of achieving your health goals easy, delicious, and convenient. Having your meals and snacks consist of whole foods and simple additions that are cooked and blended makes preparation fast and fun. Further simplifying the soup cleanse is the process of storing ready-to-eat meals and snacks that makes eating your favorite meals and snacks at home or on the go quick and easy.

Less Food Waste and More Fiber

One major benefit of soup cleansing that makes it stand out from other cleanses that focus on juicing or liquids is its use of whole foods in their entirety. By using an entire food—be it a fruit, vegetable, or whole grain—the fiber content is improved immensely. With this additional fiber, the body and brain benefit in countless ways. You'll experience increased feelings of fullness that minimize hunger, any cravings will be kept at bay, your colon will be cleansed of buildup and waste, and your organs and blood will be cleansed of the toxins that accumulate over time.

It's All-Natural

Undertaking the soup cleanse also forces you to become aware of what foods go into your snacks and meals and where those foods come from. The apples, pears, berries, citrus, carrots, potatoes, celery, and greens used in the cleansing recipes in Part 2 can all be found in their whole, natural, organic forms at any local grocer, farmers' market, or even a local farm. By associating your healthy eating with the natural foods that comprise each recipe, you can improve your awareness of the satisfying delicious and nutritious aspects of whole foods, helping you to stay focused on integrating those same nutrient-dense foods into your diet long after your soup cleanse has come to an end.

It Saves You Money

By planning your soups ahead and designing a corresponding grocery list, you can save not only time but money, too! With diets and cleanses that encourage you to use "new and exciting" ingredients, you can sometimes find yourself with a refrigerator full of produce that leaves you with a hefty portion inevitably going to waste either from not being used quickly enough or from the discovery that you dislike an ingredient only after you've made the purchase. This book is designed to provide you with a wide variety of soup-cleansing recipes that you can choose to include in your personal soup cleanse program depending upon what foods you love and would enjoy including in your soups, so you buy only ingredients you love, need, and will actually use! Once your soup-cleansing preparation commences, you'll find that you use every bit of your purchased produce and additions. And with the option to freeze extra servings of your prepared soups, no soup goes to waste!

With every batch of delicious soup you create, you save money. With a fraction of your original food costs being spent on a concise list of produce and additions that create your soups, no food goes to waste. One batch of soup costs less than one average meal purchased outside the home, and every batch makes plentiful servings that can be consumed as breakfasts, lunches, dinners, and snacks for days. With every batch of soup you create, you not only improve your quality of life through better health, but also through the saving of countless dollars that would otherwise have been wasted on unused or discarded waste or unhealthy meal alternatives purchased on the go.

It Satisfies Your Appetite

The most popular cleanses of today vary widely and include the Master Cleanse, juice cleanses, sugar detoxes, colon cleanses, and fasting detoxes, among countless others. While many of these cleanses may successfully lead to weight loss or detoxification, the radical nature of their regimens that strictly limit the diet, eliminate necessary nutrients by eliminating natural nutrient-dense foods, or provide the body with extremely limited calories are notoriously difficult to adhere to and can lead to serious conditions like nausea, dizziness, excessive hunger, agitation, and even weakened immunity. Through a safer alternative like the soup cleanse, the body and mind are provided with consistent replenishment of clean nutrients that satisfy hunger, improve energy levels, support system functioning, and promote the purification of toxins and waste. And by providing the option of snacks and meals that can be consumed hot as well as cold, the soup cleanse stands out from the cleansing crowd by offering up warm meal options that some might consider "comfort foods" that can improve feelings of fullness, unlike the strictly cold cleanses that focus on cold juices, smoothies, and drinks that can leave you feeling dissatisfied.

Different from other detoxification methods that limit calories, eliminate nutrient-dense foods, and wreak havoc on the body and mind by zapping energy and focus, the soup cleanse is designed to keep you satisfied, energized, and motivated as you reach your goal of purifying and rejuvenating your body and mind. With a consistent meal plan of plentiful servings of hearty soups packed with vibrant fruits, vegetables, and nutritious additions, the soup cleanse focuses on satisfying the body's needs for nutrients and restoring a sense of balance to the body that enables the systems and cells to work at their very best. Every two to three hours, you enjoy a splendid soup of your choice that delivers nutrient-dense spoonfuls of satisfying deliciousness to your taste buds that also keeps your mind and body functioning at its best. No calorie counting, rigorous exercise routines, or energy-zapping routines and regimens are involved in the soup cleanse, so you'll happily continue living your normal life, but with health benefits that improve your quality of life gradually as you successfully purge your body and mind of toxicity . . . naturally and deliciously!

Since it's designed to keep you eating consistently throughout the day, the soup cleanse helps you to feel more energized, focused, and satisfied with fewer cravings and with fewer and less extreme low-energy points throughout the day. Not only does this steady energy support allow the soup cleanse to provide the essentials that revitalize your body and mind, but it also helps to both improve your metabolism and give you the extra energy needed to engage in regular physical activity, helping you to achieve and maintain a healthy weight.

It Supercharges Your Metabolism

The metabolic functioning that dictates our energy level and weight gets supercharged with the soup cleanse's consistent schedule of meals every two to three hours, providing the body with ample amounts of clean "fuel" to burn that also negates the body's natural tendency to horde fat when placed on the restrictive diet of most cleanses. This bump in metabolic functioning also leads to weight loss, which is among the most commonly reported results of soup cleanse users. With an improved metabolism, increased nutrition availability, and energy levels that exceed anything experienced before, soup cleanse users adopt a healthy lifestyle that improves the chances of integrating and sustaining healthy lifestyle habits that can and will improve your health and quality of life for good! While following the routine of the soup cleanse, the healthy habits of eating clean foods, eating consistently throughout the day, and performing regular physical activity become easier to assimilate into your life permanently.

It Improves Your Skin, Hair, and Nails

Aesthetically, the benefits of the soup cleanse are beyond compare! Your skin, hair, and nails, once under a constant barrage of toxins, will appear healthier once you make the simple changes to your normal routine that are required by the soup cleanse. The essential beauty nutrients like vitamins

A, Bs, C, and E; minerals like calcium, magnesium, iron, and silica; and a variety of antioxidants that are required for optimal health can be hard to find in the Standard American Diet. When these nutrients are supplied through the specifically designed combinations of fruits, vegetables, and additions (like Greek yogurt, kefir, nuts, and seeds) that are included in the aesthetically geared soup recipes of this book, the benefits not only improve the quality of the skin but improve the texture and health of hair, the health of the eyes, and the strength of the nails. Seemingly unimportant, these aesthetic improvements signify a major improvement of health within the body, supporting the success of the soup cleanse in not only the way you feel but also the way you look!

It Helps the Liver

Giving the liver, the organ tasked with removing toxins from the body, a much-deserved rest from its busy job with a normally toxin-filled diet, the soup cleanse allows the liver to re-establish its health and return to work stronger, healthier, and more efficient than ever before. Delivering vitamins, minerals, enzymes, probiotics, and powerful phytochemicals that improve immunity, fight toxins, and help purge the body and brain of toxicity, the soup cleanse utilizes whole-food ingredients like fruits, vegetables, yogurts, nuts, and seeds that improve overall health and minimize the work required from the liver even more!

It Boosts Immune System Functioning

The soup cleanse, with its maximized delivery of supercharged nutrients, also benefits the immune system. With the inclusion of vitamins, minerals, antioxidants, and phytochemicals, in addition to the protein, carbohydrates, and fats that are essential for a strong immune system, the soup cleanse provides the immune system with all it needs and nothing it doesn't. By delivering these nutrients and phytochemicals to the body in every single soup serving, the naturally occurring vitamins, minerals, enzymes, and phytochemicals can improve the detoxification process by ridding the body and brain of harmful toxins and assisting the immune system by improving overall health and minimizing the workload of the immune system.

It Helps the Cardiovascular System

With the soup cleanse, the cardio-vascular system is given a clean diet free of toxicity, which helps minimize the very assailants that can wreak havoc on the blood and entire cardiovascular system. For example, assailants like cholesterol and triglycerides can contribute to the development of high levels of "bad" cholesterol (LDL) and plaque that minimizes blood flow through the arteries. The soup cleanse's whole foods, which are rich in iron, potassium, magnesium, and B vitamins, combine to cleanse the blood, which promotes the health of all organs and systems that receive nutrients via the bloodstream. It also promotes heart health with a low-fat, low-cholesterol, blood-sugar-regulating, hormone-balancing healthy blast of nutrition consistently.

It Regulates Your Blood Sugar

The blood sugar regulation that results from eating consistent bowls of soup throughout the day not only helps the body and brain to maintain healthy levels of nutrients, but it also helps maintain consistent energy levels and improves cognitive functioning. With the low glycemic index of the whole fruits and vegetables packed into every one of these soups, every snack and meal helps your body maintain a normal, healthy blood sugar level, as opposed to high-glycemic foods (sugar, processed foods, and refined carbohydrates, for example) that spike blood sugar and result in an inevitable drop. With this steadying of blood sugar levels, you can avoid low energy dips, mental fogginess, irritability, and cravings that can lead to overeating and weight gain.

It's Fiber-Filled

As mentioned earlier in this chapter, the soup cleanse is detoxifying because it includes fiber-rich fruits and vegetables to assist the purging of waste and undigested food particles in the digestive system that can complicate digestion, interfere with nutrient absorption, and cause serious conditions and diseases. And it also provides the body with countless protective phytonutrients that support and safeguard the body's cells and systems. The fiber-filled soup cleanse is able to help every aspect of the body's functioning with the ease of a delicious diet that satisfies for the entire duration.

With fiber-rich ingredients like fruits and vegetables and delicious additions like flax and chia seeds, the soup cleanse provides the body with natural sources of indigestible plant fibers that form a fibrous jelly that sweeps through the digestive tract, collecting and cleansing the entire digestive system of particles of undigested waste and debris. Not only does getting rid of this potentially toxic debris help safeguard your digestive system against toxicity, illness, and disease, but your cleaner colon also helps to improve the efficiency and health of your digestive system, which results in more regular, more efficient, and more comfortable bowel movements.

Attacking toxins with potent antioxidants, supplying the body's cells and systems with maximized nutrition, and digesting fiber-rich fruits and vegetables that purge the digestive system of waste and debris, the soup cleanse is the safe detoxifying option that won't leave you tired, hungry, or longing for the end. While you take the time to savor the flavors of delightfully delicious and nutritious creations, your body gets a well-deserved break from the plentiful toxins that are overwhelmingly packed into the Standard American Diet. But what do you need to have on hand in order to start enjoying the benefits—and taste!—of the soup cleanse? Read on!

Souping Necessities

With a little bit of time, a grocery list of ingredients, a variety of glass storage containers, and some handy kitchen tools you probably already have in your kitchen, you can start your soup cleansing and be well on your way to a healthier life as early as today! The first step is to prep your kitchen to make sure you have what you need on hand. Some souping essentials include:

- Large pot (able to hold at least 16 cups of water): A metal, steel, or cast-iron pot with a tight-fitting lid is highly recommended. Able to withstand high heat without worry of chemicals being released if an immersion blender's blades or utensils scratch the surface, and easy to clean, these pots are perfect for the soup cleanse recipes in Part 2.
- Large countertop blender: Most countertop blenders are able to hold a significant amount of soup, but a blender able to hold at least 10 cups of liquid and solids is preferable. Because most recipes call for the ingredients placed in the blender to be fully broken down, it is highly recommended to use a blender rated at 500 watts or more, and that has sharp blades.
- Immersion blender: Easy to find, inexpensive, and simple to use, the immersion blender will be one of your most commonly used soup-making tools. This tool has a handle that extends into

a subtle-looking circle that provides the exterior protection against sharp interior blades. The handle allows you to submerge the blades into a pot of ingredients and blend the ingredients until the desired consistency is achieved. Look for a high-quality, easy-to-wash, easy-to-handle immersion blender with high wattage for the best results in your one-pot soup making.

- Roasting pan or baking sheet: A 13" × 9" or larger pan will be perfect for the roasting that's required for a number of these soups. A metal pan, as opposed to nonstick, is recommended out of concern for the possibility of chemicals being released from the pan into the food.
- Sharp knives for food prep: With a variety of sharp knives, you can simplify your meal prep and speed the process. With the right tools, your citrus can be peeled and your potatoes can be chopped quickly, helping you to maximize the nutrition content of your soups with ease.
- Peeler: With some ingredients, such as carrots and ginger, a peeler will be needed in order to peel away the exterior prior to including the ingredients in the soups. A simple, sharp, easy-to-handle peeler will help keep your food prep fast and fluid.
- Utensils: Spoons and forks will all help you prepare your soup, test the tenderness of ingredients while cooking, and sip your soup. By having a number of utensils on hand at home and on the go, you can ensure your soup cleanse is as easy to follow as possible.

- Glass soup containers: Glass containers are highly recommended, especially those certified as being BPA-free. Whether for storage, carrying on the go, and even reheating, glass storage containers will help keep your soups fresh and ready to eat at any time. For large batches of soup, use a 8–12-cup glass container, while small single-serving containers make for perfect all-in-one storage containers that double as on-the-go bowls. Tight-fitting lids are essential, ensuring that spills and leaks don't happen in the fridge, bag, or car.

Now that you've organized, planned, and prepped, you're ready to start souping! Through a simple and delicious plan like the soup cleanse, you can sip your way to greater health and a quality of life you may have never even dreamed possible! Enjoy!

PART 2

Healthy Souping Recipes

Now that you know why to try the soup cleanse and what you need to have on hand, it's time for you to start making healthy, delicious soups! To start, determine your health goals, decide how many soups you'll need for the number of days you choose to soup (varying from 1–3 days for a quick cleanse/detox and minor weight-/water-loss goals to soup cleanses of 5–14 days that are more appropriate for health issues such as inflammation or weight-loss goals exceeding 5 pounds), then choose the recipes that not only fit your health goal needs but also appeal to your taste buds.

In this part, you'll find more than 200 soups that include vibrant, fresh fruits and vegetables; nutritious nut milks like coconut milk; probiotic- and protein-rich dairy like kefir and Greek yogurt; and healthy additions like flaxseed, chia seeds, apple cider vinegar, and much more! Optimizing health with every sip, these delightful recipes help you design your own soup cleanse program that fits your needs and satisfies your tastes! At home or on the go, you can enjoy delicious and nutritious soups that help you achieve your health goals effortlessly. Whether you're craving sweet or savory, the vibrant fruits and savory combinations of vegetables in these soup recipes are designed to satisfy your taste buds all while fulfilling your body's requirements for essential nutrition. With the tastiness of each soup making your soup cleanse easy to follow for any number of days, you can set your goals for increasing energy, improving immunity, maximizing metabolism and weight loss, or even enhancing the appearance of your skin, hair, and nails without ever feeling deprived.

Note that achieving the perfect desired consistency is an important factor in creating the most delicious and nutritious soup-cleansing recipes for your specific palate. While the recipes included in this book have specific ingredient amounts included in order to determine the correct nutritional statistics per recipe, any time you see a liquid, you should feel free to gradually add that liquid until your desired consistency is achieved. Of course, this is only added as an option and does not need to be followed unless you find your soup too thick for your tastes.

So get your blenders ready and get ready to soup cleanse!

CHAPTER 2

Breakfast Soups

Overnight, while you sleep, your body uses the nutrients you've consumed throughout the day to satisfy the needs of the cells, organs, systems, and processes that do everything from protecting your body against illness and disease to metabolizing nutrients for energy and focus. This round-the-clock work that goes on while you sleep leaves your body in need of nutrition first thing in the morning. That's where breakfast comes into play! In this chapter, you'll find delicious and nutritious replenishing recipes that focus on ingredients such as beautiful berries, sweet apples and pears, juicy fruits, vibrant vegetables, and creamy additions, which are packed with vitamins, minerals, and powerful phytochemicals like enzymes, antioxidants, and unique oils that maximize health and help you achieve your health goals. By enjoying breakfast soups like Beautiful Blue Grains, Citrus Deliciousness, Peach Perfection, and Nectarine Cream to help your body's cells, organs, and systems function as intended, you help to maximize your metabolism, improve mental functioning, and maintain healthier functioning of your entire body by jump-starting your day with natural sugars and complex carbohydrates that not only stimulate the brain and body but help to maintain a steady blood sugar level for sustained energy and maintained mental clarity and focus. So start your day with one of these surprisingly healthy breakfast soups, and enjoy your soup cleanse, stick to it, and succeed at achieving your health goals—deliciously!

Berry Breakfast Soup

YIELDS 4 SERVINGS

2 cups blueberries

2 cups strawberries, tops removed

1 cup raspberries

5 cups purified water

1 cup freshly squeezed orange juice

1. Combine all ingredients in a countertop blender.

2. Blend on high until all ingredients are broken down and thoroughly combined, about 1–2 minutes.

3. Consume immediately, or if you prefer to eat the soup hot, transfer the desired amount of soup to a large saucepan over medium heat, stirring for about 5–7 minutes until the soup reaches a simmer. Remove from heat, allow to cool slightly, and enjoy at the desired temperature.

4. To store, transfer soup to a large glass container with a tight-fitting lid and store in the refrigerator for up to 3 days.

Per serving:
Calories: 147
Fat: 0.75 grams
Protein: 2.5 grams

Sodium: 14 milligrams
Carbohydrates: 35.8 grams
Sugar: 22.9 grams
Fiber: 8.2 grams

Beautiful Blue Grains

YIELDS 4 SERVINGS

2½ cups blueberries

2½ cups blackberries

2 cups kefir

4 cups unsweetened vanilla almond milk

2 cups cooked quinoa

1. Combine all ingredients except quinoa in a countertop blender.

2. Blend on high until ingredients are broken down and thoroughly combined, about 1 minute.

3. Transfer soup to a large glass container with a tight-fitting lid and stir in quinoa until all ingredients are thoroughly combined.

4. Consume immediately or transfer soup to a large glass container with a tight-fitting lid and store in the refrigerator for up to 3 days.

Per serving:
Calories: 392
Fat: 7.3 grams
Protein: 13.1 grams

Sodium: 233 milligrams
Carbohydrates: 66.6 grams
Sugar: 27.3 grams
Fiber: 15.8 grams

Berry Banana Breakfast

YIELDS 4 SERVINGS

2 cups strawberries, tops removed

2 cups blueberries

2 bananas, peeled and halved

2 cups vanilla Greek yogurt

4 cups vanilla almond milk

1. Combine all ingredients in a blender.

2. Blend on high until all ingredients are broken down and thoroughly combined, about 1 minute.

3. Consume immediately or transfer soup to a large glass container with a tight-fitting lid and store in the refrigerator for up to 3 days.

Per serving:
Calories: 326
Fat: 8.0 grams
Protein: 12.0 grams

Sodium: 197 milligrams
Carbohydrates: 55.7 grams
Sugar: 42.2 grams
Fiber: 5.7 grams

Banana Nut Gazpacho

YIELDS 4 SERVINGS

1 cup raw natural almonds
1 cup raw natural cashews
4 cups unsweetened vanilla almond milk
2 cups kefir
3 bananas, peeled and halved

1. Combine almonds, cashews, almond milk, and kefir in a countertop blender.

2. Blend on high until nuts are broken down and thoroughly combined, about 1 minute.

3. Add bananas to the blender and blend on high until all ingredients are thoroughly combined, about 1 minute.

4. Consume immediately or transfer soup to a large glass container with a tight-fitting lid and store in the refrigerator for up to 3 days.

THE SOUP CLEANSE MAKES BREAKFAST BETTER
With the soup cleanse's nutritious and delicious recipes, you can wake up every morning looking forward to breakfasts that combine delightful combinations of various fruits, vegetables, and additions that add energy-boosting B vitamins and essential detoxifying nutrients that not only keep you full and focused but also provide the body with ample amounts of essential nutrients so you can start your day the best way!

Per serving:
Calories: 613
Fat: 41.79 grams
Protein: 20.4 grams

Sodium: 248 milligrams
Carbohydrates: 47 grams
Sugar: 20.8 grams
Fiber: 10.3 grams

Citrus Deliciousness

YIELDS 4 SERVINGS

2 pink grapefruits, peeled and seeded
2 oranges, peeled and seeded
4 kiwis, peeled and halved
1 cup freshly squeezed orange juice
6 cups purified water

1. Combine all ingredients except water in a blender.

2. Blend on high, adding water gradually while blending, until all ingredients are broken down and thoroughly combined, about 1 minute.

3. Consume immediately, or if you prefer to eat the soup hot, transfer the desired amount of soup to a large saucepan over medium heat, stirring for about 5–7 minutes until the soup reaches a simmer. Remove from heat, allow to cool slightly, and enjoy at the desired temperature.

4. To store, transfer soup to a large glass container with a tight-fitting lid and store in the refrigerator for up to 3 days.

WHY USE PURIFIED WATER?

Surprisingly enough, not all water is created equally. While unfiltered, unpurified water is readily available, the use of this water can actually derail your goals of detoxifying your body and brain by adding metals, minerals, chlorine, and a variety of additional unexpected and undesirable toxins to your soup cleanse recipes. In order to ensure your delicious and nutritious soups are as healthy as possible, use purified water.

Per serving:
Calories: 152
Fat: 0.4 grams
Protein: 2.8 grams

Sodium: 16 milligrams
Carbohydrates: 37.4 grams
Sugar: 30.0 grams
Fiber: 5.7 grams

Apple-Cinnamon Soup

YIELDS 4 SERVINGS

3 Fuji apples, peeled and cored

3 Granny Smith apples, peeled and cored

1 tablespoon ground flaxseed

2 teaspoons ground cinnamon

½ teaspoon ground cloves

6 cups vanilla almond milk

1. Combine all ingredients in a blender.

2. Blend on high until all ingredients are broken down and thoroughly combined, about 1 minute.

3. Consume immediately, or if you prefer to eat the soup hot, transfer the desired amount of soup to a large saucepan over medium heat, stirring for about 5–7 minutes until the soup reaches a simmer. Remove from heat, allow to cool slightly, and enjoy at the desired temperature.

4. To store, transfer soup to a large glass container with a tight-fitting lid and store in the refrigerator for up to 3 days.

Per serving:
Calories: 263
Fat: 4.7 grams
Protein: 2.5 grams

Sodium: 241 milligrams
Carbohydrates: 56.5 grams
Sugar: 48.4 grams
Fiber: 4.4 grams

Sweet Greens

YIELDS 4 SERVINGS

2 cups spinach

2 Granny Smith apples, peeled and cored

2 Bartlett pears, peeled and cored

2 cups blueberries

½ tablespoon ground flaxseed

3 cups organic apple juice (not from concentrate)

3 cups purified water

1. Combine all ingredients in a blender.

2. Blend on high until all ingredients are broken down and thoroughly combined, about 1 minute.

3. Consume immediately or transfer soup to a large glass container with a tight-fitting lid and store in the refrigerator for up to 3 days.

Per serving:
Calories: 248
Fat: 3.3 grams
Protein: 5.4 grams

Sodium: 107 milligrams
Carbohydrates: 53.9 grams
Sugar: 38.0 grams
Fiber: 8.5 grams

Peach Perfection

YIELDS 4 SERVINGS

4 peaches, pitted

2 bananas, peeled and halved

½ teaspoon ground cinnamon

2 cups vanilla kefir

4 cups vanilla almond milk

1. Combine all ingredients in a blender.

2. Blend on high until all ingredients are broken down and thoroughly combined, about 1 minute.

3. Consume immediately or transfer soup to a large glass container with a tight-fitting lid and store in the refrigerator for up to 3 days.

Per serving:
Calories: 311
Fat: 7.0 grams
Protein: 7.7 grams

Sodium: 223 milligrams
Carbohydrates: 58.6 grams
Sugar: 48.0 grams
Fiber: 6.6 grams

Nectarine Cream

YIELDS 4 SERVINGS

4 nectarines, pitted and quartered

2 bananas, peeled and halved

2 cups vanilla kefir

4 cups vanilla almond milk

½ teaspoon ground cloves

1. Combine all ingredients in a countertop blender.

2. Blend on high until all ingredients are broken down and thoroughly combined, about 1 minute.

3. Consume immediately or transfer soup to a large glass container with a tight-fitting lid and store in the refrigerator for up to 3 days.

Per serving:
Calories: 305
Fat: 7.1 grams
Protein: 7.6 grams

Sodium: 223 milligrams
Carbohydrates: 56.6 grams
Sugar: 43.7 grams
Fiber: 6.3 grams

Ginger-Spiced Pears

YIELDS 4 SERVINGS

4 Bartlett pears, peeled, cored, and quartered

1 cup green grapes

½" piece of ginger, peeled and sliced

3 cups organic apple juice (not from concentrate)

3 cups purified water

1. Combine all ingredients in a countertop blender.

2. Blend on high until all ingredients are broken down and thoroughly combined, about 1 minute.

3. Consume immediately, or if you prefer to eat the soup hot, transfer the desired amount of soup to a large saucepan over medium heat, stirring for about 5–7 minutes until the soup reaches a simmer. Remove from heat, allow to cool slightly, and enjoy at the desired temperature.

4. To store, transfer soup to a large glass container with a tight-fitting lid and store in the refrigerator for up to 3 days.

Per serving:
Calories: 127
Fat: 0.2 grams
Protein: 0.7 grams

Sodium: 15 milligrams
Carbohydrates: 31.9 grams
Sugar: 26.8 grams
Fiber: 1.0 grams

Citrus-Berry

YIELDS 4 SERVINGS

2 cups roughly chopped pineapple

1 cup strawberries, tops removed

1 cup blueberries

1 banana, peeled and halved

2 cups organic apple juice (not from concentrate)

4 cups purified water

1. Combine all ingredients in a countertop blender.

2. Blend on high until all ingredients are broken down and thoroughly combined, about 1 minute.

3. Consume immediately, or if you prefer to eat the soup hot, transfer the desired amount of soup to a large saucepan over medium heat, stirring for about 5–7 minutes until the soup reaches a simmer. Remove from heat, allow to cool slightly, and enjoy at the desired temperature.

4. To store, transfer soup to a large glass container with a tight-fitting lid and store in the refrigerator for up to 3 days.

ANTHOCYANINS

The deep blue hue of blueberries and blackberries results from rich concentrations of anthocyanins, phytochemicals that not only act as coloring compounds but do double duty as potent antioxidants that protect the body's cells against damage from environmental toxins, illnesses, and even cancerous cellular changes. With ample amounts of these beautiful berries added to your everyday diet with the soup cleanse, every cell, organ, and system in the body will benefit!

Per serving:
Calories: 184
Fat: 0.4 grams
Protein: 1.7 grams

Sodium: 16 milligrams
Carbohydrates: 46.9 grams
Sugar: 34.4 grams
Fiber: 4.7 grams

Berry Bomb

YIELDS 4 SERVINGS

1 cup strawberries, tops removed

1 cup blueberries

1 cup blackberries

2 kiwis, peeled and halved

1 banana, peeled and halved

2 cups freshly squeezed orange juice

4 cups purified water

1. Combine all ingredients except water in a blender.

2. Blend on high, gradually adding water until ingredients are broken down and thoroughly combined, about 1 minute.

3. Consume immediately, or if you prefer to eat the soup hot, transfer the desired amount of soup to a large saucepan over medium heat, stirring for about 5–7 minutes until the soup reaches a simmer. Remove from heat, allow to cool slightly, and enjoy at the desired temperature.

4. To store, transfer soup to a large glass container with a tight-fitting lid and store in the refrigerator for up to 3 days.

BERRIES FOR BREAKFAST

With natural sugars, sweet berries make for the perfect energy-boosting breakfast soup ingredients. Sweet, delicious, and packed with essential vitamins, minerals, and antioxidants such as anthocyanins and anthocyanadins, these beautiful powerhouses can help you start your day with a pep in your step. Adding filling fiber to any soup, berries make for the perfect ingredient for a breakfast that will not only keep you energized but also keep you satisfied for hours!

Per serving:
Calories: 168
Fat: 0.7 grams
Protein: 3.0 grams

Sodium: 12 milligrams
Carbohydrates: 40.5 grams
Sugar: 26.9 grams
Fiber: 7.0 grams

Sparkling Grape Gazpacho

YIELDS 4 SERVINGS

2 cups red grapes, pitted

2 cups green grapes, pitted

1 Bartlett pear, peeled, cored, and quartered

1 kiwi, peeled and halved

½" piece of ginger, peeled and sliced

2 cups organic apple juice (not from concentrate)

4 cups purified water

1. Combine all ingredients except water in a blender.

2. Blend on high until all ingredients are broken down and thoroughly combined, about 1 minute.

3. While blending, add water gradually.

4. Consume immediately, or if you prefer to eat the soup hot, transfer the desired amount of soup to a large saucepan over medium heat, stirring for about 5–7 minutes until the soup reaches a simmer. Remove from heat, allow to cool slightly, and enjoy at the desired temperature.

5. To store, transfer soup to a large glass container with a tight-fitting lid and store in the refrigerator for up to 3 days.

Per serving:
Calories: 226
Fat: 0.4 grams
Protein: 2.0 grams

Sodium: 18 milligrams
Carbohydrates: 58.2 grams
Sugar: 48.9 grams
Fiber: 2.8 grams

Sweet Kefir and Raspberry Soup

4 cups raspberries

2 bananas, peeled and halved

½ teaspoon ground cardamom

1 cup Greek yogurt

1 cup vanilla kefir

4 cups unsweetened vanilla almond milk

1. Combine all ingredients in a blender.

2. Blend on high until all ingredients are broken down and thoroughly combined, about 1 minute.

3. Consume immediately or transfer soup to a large glass container with a tight-fitting lid and store in the refrigerator for up to 3 days.

KEFIR: THE PERFECT PROBIOTIC

Kefir is a yogurt-like drink that can be the perfect creamy addition to soups. With plenty of probiotic bacteria that help soothe stomachaches, fight bad bacteria in the digestive system, and promote immune system functioning, kefir is a tasty addition to your soup cleanse that promotes health and well-being throughout the body!

Per serving:
Calories: 290
Fat: 8.2 grams
Protein: 10.9 grams

Sodium: 211 milligrams
Carbohydrates: 46.9 grams
Sugar: 22.4 grams
Fiber: 17.3 grams

Sweet Cinnamon Oats

YIELDS 4 SERVINGS

1 cup rolled oats

1 teaspoon ground cinnamon

4 cups vanilla almond milk

2 bananas, peeled and halved

2 cups kefir

1. Combine oats, cinnamon, and almond milk in a blender and blend on high until oats and almond milk are thoroughly combined, about 30 seconds.

2. Add bananas and kefir and blend on high until ingredients are broken down and thoroughly combined, about 1 minute.

3. Consume immediately or transfer soup to a large glass container with a tight-fitting lid and store in the refrigerator for up to 3 days.

Per serving:
Calories: 312
Fat: 6.0 grams
Protein: 9.5 grams

Sodium: 223 milligrams
Carbohydrates: 52.4 grams
Sugar: 29.2 grams
Fiber: 5.8 grams

Cantaloupe Cream

YIELDS 3 SERVINGS

4 cups cubed cantaloupe

2 bananas, peeled and halved

2 cups Greek yogurt

4 cups vanilla almond milk

1. Combine all ingredients in a blender.

2. Blend on high until all ingredients are broken down and thoroughly combined, about 1 minute.

3. Consume immediately or transfer soup to a large glass container with a tight-fitting lid and store in the refrigerator for up to 3 days.

Per serving:
Calories: 389
Fat: 10.5 grams
Protein: 16.0 grams

Sodium: 294 milligrams
Carbohydrates: 62.0 grams
Sugar: 53.1 grams
Fiber: 4.0 grams

Minty Melon

YIELDS 4 SERVINGS

2½ cups cubed cantaloupe

2½ cups cubed honeydew melon

¼" piece of ginger, peeled and sliced

2 tablespoons chopped fresh mint leaves

2 cups organic apple juice (not from concentrate)

4 cups coconut milk

1. Combine all ingredients in a countertop blender and blend on high until all ingredients are broken down and thoroughly combined, about 1 minute.

2. Consume immediately, or if you prefer to eat the soup hot, transfer the desired amount of soup to a large saucepan over medium heat, stirring for about 5–7 minutes until the soup reaches a simmer. Remove from heat, allow to cool slightly, and enjoy at the desired temperature.

3. To store, transfer soup to a large glass container with a tight-fitting lid and store in the refrigerator for up to 3 days.

Per serving:

Calories: 199

Fat: 5.3 grams

Protein: 1.3 grams

Sodium: 68 milligrams

Carbohydrates: 36.5 grams

Sugar: 32.6 grams

Fiber: 1.8 grams

Spiced Cherry Chai

YIELDS 4 SERVINGS

5 cups cherries, pitted

1 Fuji apple, peeled, cored, and quartered

½" piece of ginger, peeled and sliced

2 teaspoons ground cardamom

1 teaspoon ground cinnamon

½ teaspoon ground cloves

2 cups organic apple juice (not from concentrate)

4 cups purified water

1. Combine all ingredients in a blender.

2. Blend on high until all ingredients are broken down and thoroughly combined, about 1 minute.

3. Consume immediately, or if you prefer to eat the soup hot, transfer the desired amount of soup to a large saucepan over medium heat, stirring for about 5–7 minutes until the soup reaches a simmer. Remove from heat, allow to cool slightly, and enjoy at the desired temperature.

4. To store, transfer soup to a large glass container with a tight-fitting lid and store in the refrigerator for up to 3 days.

Per serving:

Calories: 204

Fat: 0.5 grams

Protein: 2.5 grams

Sodium: 14 milligrams

Carbohydrates: 51.8 grams

Sugar: 40.7 grams

Fiber: 5.6 grams

Fruity Chai

YIELDS 4 SERVINGS

2 bananas, peeled and halved

2 Fuji apples, peeled, cored, and quartered

2 Bartlett pears, peeled, cored, and quartered

1 teaspoon ground cardamom

1 teaspoon ground cinnamon

6 cups unsweetened vanilla almond milk

1. Combine all ingredients in a blender.

2. Blend on high until all ingredients are broken down and thoroughly combined, about 1 minute.

3. Consume immediately, or if you prefer to eat the soup hot, transfer the desired amount of soup to a large saucepan over medium heat, stirring for about 5–7 minutes until the soup reaches a simmer. Remove from heat, allow to cool slightly, and enjoy at the desired temperature.

4. To store, transfer soup to a large glass container with a tight-fitting lid and store in the refrigerator for up to 3 days.

Per serving:

Calories: 139	Sodium: 240 milligrams
Fat: 3.9 grams	Carbohydrates: 24.6 grams
Protein: 2.4 grams	Sugar: 15.4 grams
	Fiber: 3.1 grams

Quick Berry Breakfast

YIELDS 3 SERVINGS

1½ cups strawberries, tops removed

1½ cups blueberries

1 cup raspberries

1 banana, peeled and halved

1 cup peeled and chopped pineapple

6 cups unsweetened coconut milk

1. Combine all ingredients in a blender.

2. Blend on high until all ingredients are broken down and thoroughly combined, about 1 minute.

3. Consume immediately, or if you prefer to eat the soup hot, transfer the desired amount of soup to a large saucepan over medium heat, stirring for about 5–7 minutes until the soup reaches a simmer. Remove from heat, allow to cool slightly, and enjoy at the desired temperature.

4. Store soup in a large glass container with a tight-fitting lid for up to 3 days in the refrigerator.

Per serving:

Calories: 291	Sodium: 73 milligrams
Fat: 8.9 grams	Carbohydrates: 50.4 grams
Protein: 3.1 grams	Sugar: 30.7 grams
	Fiber: 11.3 grams

CHAPTER 3

Detoxifying Soups

Most people are in need of detoxification, whether they know it or not. Having grown accustomed to the very symptoms that indicate a need for a detox, the average person accepts chronic fatigue, stubborn weight gain, mental fogginess, aches and pains, and multiple systemic issues as the norm. But you can improve a life with any of these issues quickly and easily by focusing on a variety of whole foods that flush toxins out of the body and provide the entire body with essential nutrition that helps relieve pain, maximizes metabolism, increases energy, and improves immunity.

Fortunately, the nutrient-dense soups found in this chapter not only taste great, but they help you rid your body of the environmental and lifestyle elements like pollution, alcohol, and inflammatory agents that wreak havoc on your cells and systems. The ingredients in these recipes—like fruits, vegetables, yogurts, and additions like ginger, garlic, apple cider vinegar, and coconut oil—pack detoxifying and purifying enzymes and phytochemicals that, along with the immunity-boosting nutrients that further support the health of the organs directly responsible for detoxifying the body and brain like the liver and kidneys, help to purge and protect the body of toxins and hazardous elements. So if you're ready to improve your health and quality of life, enjoy sipping the flavors of detoxifying soups like the Hot and Sour Soup, Ginger-Infused Rice Noodles and Scallions, Sweet Spiced Pumpkin, and many more found in this chapter that all help you get your body and mind free of toxicity and back on track!

Hot and Sour Soup

YIELDS 4 SERVINGS

8 cups purified water

½ cup apple cider vinegar

1 tablespoon maple syrup

1 (16-ounce) package rice noodles

2 eggs

1 cup chopped scallions

1. In a large pot, combine water, apple cider vinegar, and maple syrup.

2. Over high heat, bring soup to a boil, reduce heat to a simmer, and add noodles.

3. Allow soup to simmer for about 5 minutes, stirring regularly.

4. In a separate small bowl, beat eggs. Drizzle eggs into soup and stir to develop egg ribbons.

5. Add scallions.

6. Remove from heat and allow to cool.

7. Consume immediately or transfer soup to a large glass container with a tight-fitting lid. Soup can be stored in the refrigerator for up to 5 days, or in the freezer for up to 1 month.

Per serving:

Calories: 456

Fat: 3.2 grams

Protein: 9.5 grams

Sodium: 102 milligrams

Carbohydrates: 94.2 grams

Sugar: 2.8 grams

Fiber: 0.5 grams

Spicy Radish-Kale

YIELDS 4 SERVINGS

8 cups purified water

1½ cups finely sliced radishes

3 cups chopped kale

¼ teaspoon cayenne pepper

1. In a large pot, combine water and radishes.

2. Over high heat, bring soup to a boil, reduce heat to a simmer, and cover.

3. Allow soup to simmer for 20–30 minutes.

4. Add kale, cover, and simmer for 10–15 minutes or until kale is tender.

5. Remove from heat, add cayenne, stir, and allow to cool.

6. Consume immediately or transfer soup to a large glass container with a tight-fitting lid. Soup can be stored in the refrigerator for up to 5 days or in the freezer for up to 1 month.

KILLER KALE!

Kale has long been seen as a bitter green that can be added to only specific salads, snacks, or soups, but the truth is that cooking kale softens the leaves, enhances the natural nonbitter flavors, and improves the health benefits of any snack or meal that includes this vegetable. The soups that include this deep-green vegetable have high amounts of vitamins A and K, iron, fiber, and antioxidant levels for better health benefits, with rich flavor too! Keeping in mind that fiber and antioxidants protect the entire body and the brain against unhealthy cellular changes and toxicity, anyone can see why healthy doses of kale spell healthy detoxification at its finest!

Per serving:
Calories: 32
Fat: 0.3 grams
Protein: 2.0 grams

Sodium: 57 milligrams
Carbohydrates: 6.6 grams
Sugar: 0.8 grams
Fiber: 1.7 grams

Leek, Tomato, Celery

YIELDS 4 SERVINGS

2 tablespoons extra-virgin olive oil

2 cups chopped leeks

4 celery ribs, chopped

8 cups purified water

3 Roma tomatoes, sliced and halved

1. In a large pot over medium heat, combine oil, leeks, and celery and stir for 8–10 minutes or until vegetables are softened.

2. Add water, increase heat to high, bring soup to a boil, reduce heat to a simmer, and cover.

3. Allow soup to simmer for 20 minutes.

4. Add tomatoes, cover, and simmer for 5 minutes.

5. Remove from heat and allow to cool.

6. Consume immediately or transfer soup to a large glass container with a tight-fitting lid. Soup can be stored in the refrigerator for up to 5 days or in the freezer for up to 1 month.

Per serving:
Calories: 111
Fat: 6.9 grams
Protein: 1.8 grams

Sodium: 134 milligrams
Carbohydrates: 11.0 grams
Sugar: 4.7 grams
Fiber: 3.2 grams

Sweet Pea, Broccoli, and Vidalia

YIELDS 4 SERVINGS

8 cups purified water

2 cups chopped Vidalia onions

2 cups fresh sweet peas (may also use frozen and thawed)

2 cups broccoli florets

1. In a large pot, combine water and onions.

2. Over high heat, bring soup to a boil, reduce heat to a simmer, and cover.

3. Allow soup to simmer for 10 minutes.

4. Add peas and broccoli, cover, and simmer for 5 minutes.

5. Remove from heat and allow to cool for 5 minutes.

6. Using an immersion blender, blend on high until all ingredients are broken down and a smooth consistency is achieved, about 2–3 minutes.

7. Consume immediately or transfer soup to a large glass container with a tight-fitting lid. Soup can be stored in the refrigerator for up to 5 days or in the freezer for up to 1 month.

Per serving:
Calories: 150
Fat: 0.6 grams
Protein: 10.3 grams

Sodium: 61 milligrams
Carbohydrates: 28.7 grams
Sugar: 10.5 grams
Fiber: 6.6 grams

Ginger-Infused Rice Noodles and Scallions

YIELDS 4 SERVINGS

8 cups purified water
2" piece of ginger, peeled and grated
2 cups chopped scallions
1 (16-ounce) package rice noodles

1. In a large pot, combine water, ginger, and scallions.

2. Over high heat, bring soup to a boil, reduce heat to a simmer, and cover.

3. Allow soup to simmer for 15–20 minutes or until ginger is tender.

4. Add rice noodles and stir until noodles are tender, about 1–2 minutes.

5. Remove from heat and allow to cool.

6. Consume immediately or transfer soup to a large glass container with a tight-fitting lid. Soup can be stored in the refrigerator for up to 5 days or in the freezer for up to 1 month.

Per serving:
Calories: 415
Fat: 1.08 grams
Protein: 6.8 grams

Sodium: 69 milligrams
Carbohydrates: 93.6 grams
Sugar: 0.9 grams
Fiber: 1.0 grams

Spiced Clean Greens

YIELDS 4 SERVINGS

8 cups purified water

1 cup chopped red onions

2 garlic cloves, grated

1 tablespoon curry powder

1 tablespoon ground turmeric

3 cups chopped kale

3 cups chopped spinach

1. In a large pot, combine water, red onion, garlic, curry, and turmeric.

2. Over high heat, bring soup to a boil, reduce heat to a simmer, and cover.

3. Allow soup to simmer for 10 minutes.

4. Add kale and spinach and simmer for 10–15 minutes.

5. Remove from heat and allow to cool.

6. Consume immediately or transfer soup to a large glass container with a tight-fitting lid. Soup can be stored in the refrigerator for up to 5 days or in the freezer for up to 1 month.

SPINACH FOR SPLENDID SOUP RECIPES

With the addition of light-tasting spinach, soups get improved nutritional content that includes not only vitamins A, C, E, and K and minerals like iron, calcium, and magnesium, but also detoxifying fiber and antioxidants as well as unique phytochemicals that help purge toxins and protect everything from blood health and digestion to immune system functioning.

Per serving:
Calories: 97
Fat: 1.0 grams
Protein: 7.6 grams

Sodium: 179 milligrams
Carbohydrates: 18.3 grams
Sugar: 2.6 grams
Fiber: 6.6 grams

Beany Greens

YIELDS 4 SERVINGS

8 cups purified water

1 cup chopped red onions

2 cups canned garbanzo beans (may also use dried beans that have been soaked for 24 hours)

2 cups chopped spinach

2 cups chopped kale

1 teaspoon ground black pepper

1. In a large pot, combine water, onion, and garbanzo beans.

2. Over high heat, bring soup to a boil, reduce heat to a simmer, and cover.

3. Allow soup to simmer for 20 minutes.

4. Add spinach and kale and simmer for 10–15 minutes.

5. Remove from heat, add pepper, and allow to cool.

6. Consume immediately or transfer soup to a large glass container with a tight-fitting lid. Soup can be stored in the refrigerator for up to 5 days or in the freezer for up to 1 month.

THE POWER OF VITAMIN K

Greens deliver rich amounts of vitamin K, which is a fat-soluble vitamin your body needs for a number of bodily functions. Required for proper blood clotting, vitamin K also protects against osteoporosis and tooth decay, aids in the processing and storage of minerals throughout the body, and helps protect against illness and disease. Boosting this vitamin's health-protecting potential is its ability to support the process of removing toxins from the blood while also supporting the major organs responsible for detoxifying the brain and body: the digestive system, kidneys, and liver.

Per serving:
Calories: 165
Fat: 2.6 grams
Protein: 10.2 grams

Sodium: 312 milligrams
Carbohydrates: 28.7
Sugar: 5.2 grams
Fiber: 8.9 grams

Three Beans, Wild Rice, and Spinach

YIELDS 4 SERVINGS

8 cups purified water

2 cloves garlic, grated

1 cup canned garbanzo beans (may also use dried beans that have been soaked for 24 hours)

1 cup canned black beans (may also use dried beans that have been soaked for 24 hours)

1 cup canned red pinto beans (may also use dried beans that have been soaked for 24 hours)

2 cups cooked wild rice

4 cups chopped spinach

1. In a large pot, combine water, garlic, and all beans.

2. Over high heat, bring soup to a boil, reduce heat to a simmer, and cover.

3. Allow soup to simmer for 20 minutes.

4. Add rice and spinach and stir for 2–3 minutes or until spinach is wilted.

5. Remove from heat and allow to cool.

6. Consume immediately or transfer soup to a large glass container with a tight-fitting lid. Soup can be stored in the refrigerator for up to 5 days or in the freezer for up to 1 month.

Per serving:
Calories: 296
Fat: 2.0 grams
Protein: 20.1 grams

Sodium: 467 milligrams
Carbohydrates: 53.6 grams
Sugar: 4.4 grams
Fiber: 15.5 grams

Split Pea, Sweet Potato, and Spinach

YIELDS 4 SERVINGS

8 cups purified water

2 cups split peas

2 large sweet potatoes, scrubbed and cubed into ¼" chunks

3 cups chopped spinach

1. In a large pot, combine water and split peas.

2. Over high heat, bring soup to a boil, reduce heat to a simmer, and cover.

3. Allow soup to simmer for 45 minutes.

4. Add sweet potato and simmer for 20 minutes or until fork-tender.

5. Add spinach and stir for 2–3 minutes or until spinach is wilted.

6. Remove from heat and allow to cool.

7. Consume immediately or transfer soup to a large glass container with a tight-fitting lid. Soup can be stored in the refrigerator for up to 5 days or in the freezer for up to 1 month.

Per serving:
Calories: 233
Fat: 0.7 grams
Protein: 14.5 grams

Sodium: 206 milligrams
Carbohydrates: 45.3 grams
Sugar: 7.4 grams
Fiber: 14.7 grams

Creamy Kale and Spinach

YIELDS 4 SERVINGS

8 cups unsweetened almond milk

3 garlic cloves, grated

3 cups chopped kale

3 cups chopped spinach

1 teaspoon ground black pepper

1. In a large pot, combine almond milk, garlic, kale, and spinach.

2. Over high heat, bring soup to a boil, reduce heat to a simmer, and cover.

3. Allow soup to simmer for 10–15 minutes or until kale is tender.

4. Remove from heat, add pepper, and allow to cool.

5. Using an immersion blender, submerge blades and blend on high until all ingredients are broken down and well combined.

6. Consume immediately or transfer soup to a large glass container with a tight-fitting lid. Soup can be stored in the refrigerator for up to 5 days or in the freezer for up to 1 month.

IRON FOR OPTIMAL HEALTH

While iron is an essential mineral that helps maintain optimal blood health, it is also essential in energy production. Without ample amounts of iron—found in abundance in leafy greens like spinach and kale—it is common to experience frequent bouts of fatigue and mental fogginess. Known as a nutrient essential for blood health, iron supports the body's natural toxin-removing process by not only supporting a healthy cardiovascular system but also by keeping the blood and all organs functioning at their best and detoxifying the body and brain as intended. By consuming 2–3 cups of leafy greens daily, you can deliver proper doses of this essential mineral to your body for better focus, energy, and health!

Per serving:
Calories: 141
Fat: 5.7 grams
Protein: 9.3 grams

Sodium: 479 milligrams
Carbohydrates: 15.2 grams
Sugar: 0.8 grams
Fiber: 5.2 grams

Garden Medley

YIELDS 4 SERVINGS

8 cups purified water

1 garlic clove, minced

2 carrots, ends removed, peeled, and chopped

3 celery stalks, chopped

2 small yellow potatoes, chopped

1 cup chopped red onions

1 cup sweet green peas

1. In a large pot, combine water, garlic, carrot, celery, potato, and onion.

2. Over high heat, bring soup to a boil, reduce heat to a simmer, and cover.

3. Allow soup to simmer for 20 minutes.

4. Add peas and simmer for 5 minutes.

5. Remove from heat and allow to cool.

6. Consume immediately or transfer soup to a large glass container with a tight-fitting lid. Soup can be stored in the refrigerator for up to 5 days or in the freezer for up to 1 month.

Per serving:

Calories: 175

Fat: 0.5 grams

Protein: 6.8 grams

Sodium: 128 milligrams

Carbohydrates: 37.3 grams

Sugar: 8.9 grams

Fiber: 7.5 grams

Thyme, Turmeric, Broccoli, and Spinach

YIELDS 4 SERVINGS

8 cups purified water

2 cups broccoli florets

2 cups chopped spinach

2 tablespoons dried thyme

1 tablespoon ground turmeric

2 garlic cloves, grated

1. In a large pot, combine all ingredients.

2. Over high heat, bring soup to a boil, reduce heat to a simmer, and cover.

3. Allow soup to simmer for 15 minutes.

4. Remove from heat and allow to cool.

5. Consume immediately or transfer soup to a large glass container with a tight-fitting lid. Soup can be stored in the refrigerator for up to 5 days or in the freezer for up to 1 month.

Per serving:

Calories: 73

Fat: 0.8 grams

Protein: 7.2 grams

Sodium: 142 milligrams

Carbohydrates: 13.4 grams

Sugar: 0.6 grams

Fiber: 3.6 grams

Vegetable Noodle

YIELDS 4 SERVINGS

8 cups purified water

2 carrots, ends removed, peeled, and chopped

3 celery stalks, chopped

2 cups chopped yellow onions

1 cup fresh sweet peas (may also use frozen and thawed)

1 cup fresh corn kernels (may also use frozen and thawed)

1 (16-ounce) package rice noodles

1. In a large pot, combine water, carrots, celery, and onion.
2. Over high heat, bring soup to a boil, reduce heat to a simmer, and cover.
3. Allow soup to simmer for 10 minutes.
4. Add peas and corn and simmer for 10 minutes.
5. Add rice noodles and stir until noodles are tender, about 2 minutes.
6. Remove from heat and allow to cool.
7. Consume immediately or transfer soup to a large glass container with a tight-fitting lid. Soup can be stored in the refrigerator for up to 5 days or in the freezer for up to 1 month.

Per serving:
Calories: 542
Fat: 1.7 grams
Protein: 12.1 grams

Sodium: 172 milligrams
Carbohydrates: 120.1 grams
Sugar: 11.4 grams
Fiber: 7.9 grams

Broccoli, Spinach, and Spirulina

YIELDS 4 SERVINGS

8 cups purified water

3 cups broccoli florets

3 cups chopped spinach

3 garlic cloves, grated

2 tablespoons spirulina

1. In a large pot, combine water, broccoli, spinach, and garlic.

2. Over high heat, bring soup to a boil, reduce heat to a simmer, and cover.

3. Allow soup to simmer for 15 minutes.

4. Remove from heat and stir in spirulina, blending well. Allow to cool.

5. Consume immediately or transfer soup to a large glass container with a tight-fitting lid. Soup can be stored in the refrigerator for up to 5 days or in the freezer for up to 1 month.

SWEET GREENS

When you add greens to your favorite soup recipes, the cooking process may change the way you look at nutritious vegetables. When fiber-rich, detoxifying greens—packed with vitamin K, iron, and magnesium that all contribute to the detoxification processes—such as spinach, kale, and collards are cooked in soups, the heat and the addition of flavorful ingredients and liquids can transform the flavors of greens from bitter to subtle or even slightly sweet.

Per serving:

Calories: 103

Fat: 1.0 grams

Protein: 12.3 grams

Sodium: 238 milligrams

Carbohydrates: 17.3 grams

Sugar: 0.9 grams

Fiber: 4.0 grams

Quinoa Vegetable

YIELDS 4 SERVINGS

8 cups purified water

2 carrots, ends removed, peeled, and chopped

1 cup chopped red onions

2 zucchini, ends removed and chopped

2 yellow squash, ends removed and chopped

2 cups cooked quinoa

1. In a large pot, combine water, carrot, and onion.

2. Over high heat, bring soup to a boil, reduce heat to a simmer, and cover.

3. Allow soup to simmer for 20 minutes.

4. Add zucchini and yellow squash and simmer 5 minutes.

5. Remove from heat, stir in quinoa, and allow to cool.

6. Consume immediately or transfer soup to a large glass container with a tight-fitting lid. Soup can be stored in the refrigerator for up to 5 days or in the freezer for up to 1 month.

Per serving:
Calories: 198
Fat: 0.5 grams
Protein: 8.2 grams

Sodium: 59 milligrams
Carbohydrates: 37.4 grams
Sugar: 7.8 grams
Fiber: 6.8 grams

Sweet Spiced Pumpkin

YIELDS 4 SERVINGS

2 tablespoons coconut oil

4 cups ¼"-cubed pumpkin

1 tablespoon maple syrup

2 tablespoons ground cinnamon

1 tablespoon ground cloves

1" piece of ginger, peeled and grated

8 cups purified water

1. In a large pot over medium heat, combine coconut oil, pumpkin, maple syrup, cinnamon, cloves, and ginger. Sauté for 5 minutes, then cover with water.

2. Over high heat, bring soup to a boil, reduce heat to a simmer, and cover.

3. Allow soup to simmer for 30 minutes.

4. Remove from heat and allow to cool.

5. Consume immediately or transfer soup to a large glass container with a tight-fitting lid. Soup can be stored in the refrigerator for up to 5 days or in the freezer for up to 1 month.

Per serving:

Calories: 150	Sodium: 25 milligrams
Fat: 6.9 grams	Carbohydrates: 23.3 grams
Protein: 2.8 grams	Sugar: 5.5 grams
	Fiber: 4.1 grams

Apple, Pear, and Squash Soup

YIELDS 4 SERVINGS

2 Fuji apples, peeled, cored, and cubed into ¼" cubes

2 Bartlett pears, peeled, cored, and cubed into ¼" cubes

2 acorn squash, peeled, seeded, and cubed into ¼" cubes

1 tablespoon ground cloves

8 cups purified water

1. In a large pot, combine apples, pears, squash, and cloves and cover with water.

2. Over high heat, bring soup to a boil, reduce heat to a simmer, and cover.

3. Allow soup to simmer for 15 minutes or until all ingredients are fork-tender.

4. Remove from heat and allow to cool.

5. Consume immediately or transfer soup to a large glass container with a tight-fitting lid. Soup can be stored in the refrigerator for up to 5 days or in the freezer for up to 1 month.

Per serving:

Calories: 129	Sodium: 29 milligrams
Fat: 0.5 grams	Carbohydrates: 33.8 grams
Protein: 2.0 grams	Sugar: 8.2 grams
	Fiber: 4.6 grams

Beet-Apple Treat

YIELDS 4 SERVINGS

2 red beets, scrubbed and cubed into ¼"
cubes

2 golden beets, scrubbed and cubed into
¼" cubes

2 Granny Smith apples, peeled, cored, and
cubed into ¼" cubes

2 tablespoons ground cinnamon

8 cups purified water

1. In a large pot, combine both types of beets,
   apples, and cinnamon, then cover with water.

2. Over high heat, bring soup to a boil, reduce heat
   to a simmer, and cover.

3. Allow soup to simmer for 25–30 minutes or until
   all ingredients are fork-tender.

4. Remove from heat and allow to cool.

5. Consume immediately or transfer soup to a large
   glass container with a tight-fitting lid. Soup can
   be stored in the refrigerator for up to 5 days or in
   the freezer for up to 1 month.

Per serving:
Calories: 94
Fat: 0.2 grams
Protein: 2.0 grams

Sodium: 97 milligrams
Carbohydrates: 23.0 grams
Sugar: 15.0 grams
Fiber: 5.9 grams

Garlicky Miroqua Soup

YIELDS 4 SERVINGS

2 tablespoons extra-virgin olive oil

2 yellow onions, peeled and chopped

4 celery ribs, chopped

2 large carrots, ends removed, peeled, and chopped

4 garlic cloves, minced

6 cups purified water

1. In a large pot over medium heat, combine the olive oil, onions, celery, and carrots.

2. Stir constantly for 10–15 minutes until vegetables are soft and the onions translucent.

3. Stir in minced garlic and stir for 5 minutes.

4. Pour water into pot and increase temperature to high.

5. Bring to a boil, reduce heat to medium, and simmer for 10–15 minutes.

6. Remove from heat and allow to cool for 5 minutes before serving.

7. Consume immediately or transfer soup to a large glass container with a tight-fitting lid and store in the refrigerator for up to 3–5 days.

Per serving:
Calories: 128
Fat: 6.9 grams
Protein: 2.2 grams

Sodium: 147 milligrams
Carbohydrates: 15.2 grams
Sugar: 7.3 grams
Fiber: 4.4 grams

CHAPTER 4

Green Soups

Fiber-filled greens like spinach, kale, asparagus, broccoli, beans, peas, leeks, and spirulina have long been known to provide the body with a number of essential nutrients like vitamins A, C, E, and K; minerals like calcium, iron, magnesium, and silica; and a number of phytochemicals that act as potent antioxidants, which act to protect against harmful changes and mutations while also supporting the entire immune system's functioning. The fiber from these vibrant vegetables works to improve digestion and the immune system, ensures that regularity can be easily achieved and maintained, and even optimizes the quality of your blood and its ability to carry and distribute oxygen throughout your brain and body.

And, by enjoying one green soup a day, you can ensure that the nutrients and minerals that your body requires for everything from energy production and digestion to bone health and mental functioning are available as needed. Packed with vibrant, deep green vegetables that add iron, vitamin K, calcium, magnesium, and vitamin C, these soups help support blood health, detoxify the brain and body, support nervous system functioning, maintain mental focus and clarity, boost energy levels, and improve immunity. With delicious combinations of greens and other vegetables, the soup cleanse recipes found in this chapter, like Creamy Asparagus; Spinach, Scallion, and Spirulina; Sweet and Creamy Onion-Fennel; and Avocado Mint, allow you to create sweet and savory soups that make it easy to sip your daily servings of greens deliciously!

Luscious Leeks and Greens

YIELDS 4 SERVINGS

2 tablespoons extra-virgin olive oil

2 cups chopped leeks, cleaned thoroughly

2 cups spinach leaves

2 cups chopped kale

1 yellow onion, peeled and chopped

1 tablespoon garlic powder

1 tablespoon salt

8 cups Traditional Vegetable-Based Chicken Broth (see Chapter 10)

1. In a large pot over medium heat, heat olive oil until warmed.

2. Add all ingredients except broth and sauté until vegetables are softened, about 5–8 minutes.

3. Add broth to the pot and increase heat to high.

4. Bring soup to a boil, reduce heat to a simmer, and cover.

5. Allow soup to simmer for 1 hour or until vegetables are fork-tender.

6. Remove from heat and allow to cool.

7. Consume immediately or transfer soup to a large glass container with a tight-fitting lid and store in the refrigerator for up to 5 days.

Per serving:
Calories: 160
Fat: 8.3 grams
Protein: 5.2 grams

Sodium: 1827 milligrams
Carbohydrates: 17.1 grams
Sugar: 6.5 grams
Fiber: 2.6 grams

Creamy Asparagus

YIELDS 4 SERVINGS

8 cups unsweetened almond milk

4 cups asparagus spears

1 cup chopped Vidalia onions

1 teaspoon ground black pepper

1. In a large pot, combine almond milk, asparagus, onion, and black pepper.

2. Over high heat, bring soup to a boil, reduce heat to a simmer, and cover.

3. Allow soup to simmer for 20–30 minutes or until asparagus and onion are fork-tender.

4. Remove from heat and allow to cool for about 5 minutes.

5. Using an immersion blender, submerge blades and blend soup until all ingredients are well broken down and soup is fully blended, about 5 minutes.

6. Consume immediately or transfer soup to a large glass container with a tight-fitting lid. Soup can be stored in the refrigerator for up to 5 days or in the freezer for up to 1 month.

DETOXING TO KICK-START A HEALTHIER LIFE

When people decide to make healthy changes to their daily life, the beginning can be a struggle. As your body begins to assimilate to a new routine, the effects can range from fatigue and moodiness to actual withdrawal from substances like sugar, nicotine, caffeine, and alcohol. A detox minimizes these effects, gives your body a chance to speed up the removal of toxins, and decreases the time needed to restore and rejuvenate the body, making the transition to a healthier lifestyle easier to do and maintain.

Per serving:
Calories: 100
Fat: 5.1 grams
Protein: 5.3 grams

Sodium: 325 milligrams
Carbohydrates: 8.6 grams
Sugar: 4.5 grams
Fiber: 3.3 grams

Sweet and Creamy Onion-Fennel

YIELDS 4 SERVINGS

8 cups unsweetened almond milk

3 cups chopped fennel bulb, greens removed

2 cups chopped Vidalia onions

2 cups chopped spinach

1. In a large pot, combine almond milk, fennel, and onion.

2. Over high heat, bring soup to a boil, reduce heat to a simmer, and cover.

3. Allow soup to simmer for 20–30 minutes or until fennel and onion are fork-tender.

4. Add spinach and continue simmering for 5 minutes, stirring until spinach is wilted.

5. Remove from heat and allow to cool for about 5 minutes.

6. Using an immersion blender, submerge blades and blend soup until all ingredients are well broken down and soup is fully blended, about 5 minutes.

7. Consume immediately or transfer soup to a large glass container with a tight-fitting lid. Soup can be stored in the refrigerator for up to 5 days or in the freezer for up to 1 month.

Per serving:
Calories: 165
Fat: 5.3 grams
Protein: 8.1 grams

Sodium: 506 milligrams
Carbohydrates: 22.8 grams
Sugar: 4.5 grams
Fiber: 8.6 grams

Light and Creamy Broccolini

YIELDS 4 SERVINGS

8 cups unsweetened almond milk

3 cups chopped Broccolini

1 cup chopped Vidalia onions

1 garlic clove, chopped

1. In a large pot, combine almond milk, Broccolini, onion, and garlic.

2. Over high heat, bring soup to a boil, reduce heat to a simmer, and cover.

3. Allow soup to simmer for 20–25 minutes or until Broccolini and onion are fork-tender.

4. Remove from heat and allow to cool for 5 minutes.

5. Using an immersion blender, submerge blades and blend soup until all ingredients are well broken down and soup is fully blended, about 5 minutes.

6. Consume immediately or transfer soup to a large glass container with a tight-fitting lid. Soup can be stored in the refrigerator for up to 5 days or in the freezer for up to 1 month.

Per serving:
Calories: 97
Fat: 5.0 grams
Protein: 4.2 grams

Sodium: 345 milligrams
Carbohydrates: 7.8 grams
Sugar: 3.2 grams
Fiber: 2.0 grams

Great Greens

YIELDS 4 SERVINGS

8 cups purified water

3 cups chopped spinach

3 cups chopped kale, ribs removed

1 cup chopped green onions

1 garlic clove, chopped

1 teaspoon ground black pepper

1. In a large pot, combine water, spinach, kale, green onion, garlic, and black pepper.

2. Over high heat, bring soup to a boil, reduce heat to a simmer, and cover.

3. Allow soup to simmer for 15–20 minutes or until kale is tender.

4. Remove from heat and allow to cool for 5 minutes.

5. Using an immersion blender, submerge blades and blend soup until all ingredients are well broken down and soup is fully blended, about 5 minutes.

6. Consume immediately or transfer soup to a large glass container with a tight-fitting lid. Soup can be stored in the refrigerator for up to 5 days or in the freezer for up to 1 month.

THE TOXIC BATTLE

With toxins seeping into our body's simplest of cells, organs, and systems through the environment, food, and poor habits, the body struggles to perform its normal functions. With antibacterial and antiviral benefits, the garlic of this soup also helps to fend off the infiltration of microbes into the body's cells, blood, and organs, helping to improve the body's ability to detoxify effectively.

Per serving:
Calories: 73
Fat: 0.7 grams
Protein: 7.1 grams

Sodium: 179 milligrams
Carbohydrates: 13.4 grams
Sugar: 1.2 grams
Fiber: 5.4 grams

Spinach, Scallion, and Spirulina

YIELDS 4 SERVINGS

8 cups purified water

5 cups chopped spinach

2 cups chopped scallions

4 garlic cloves, chopped

2 tablespoons spirulina

1. In a large pot, combine water, spinach, scallions, and garlic.

2. Over high heat, bring soup to a boil, reduce heat to a simmer, and cover.

3. Allow soup to simmer for 10 minutes.

4. Remove from heat and allow to cool for 5 minutes.

5. Add spirulina. Using an immersion blender, submerge blades and blend soup until all ingredients are well broken down and soup is fully blended, about 5 minutes.

6. Consume immediately or transfer soup to a large glass container with a tight-fitting lid. Soup can be stored in the refrigerator for up to 5 days or in the freezer for up to 1 month.

FIBERFUL DETOX

Few people realize the importance of fiber in the detoxification process. When you consume fiberful fruits, vegetables, and additions, the fiber turns to a natural gooey substance in the digestive system and moves through the colon, cleansing the intestines of debris and unrelieved waste in its path. When the fiber has cleansed the colon of blockages and debris that can wreak havoc on the immune system, the result is an optimal digestive process that is able to absorb, process, store, and deliver nutrients throughout the body as intended, for better health and a healthier life.

Per serving:
Calories: 94
Fat: 0.9 grams
Protein: 11.2 grams

Sodium: 288 milligrams
Carbohydrates: 15.4 grams
Sugar: 2.2 grams
Fiber: 7.5 grams

Kale-Potato

YIELDS 4 SERVINGS

8 cups purified water

3 cups chopped kale, ribs removed

2 baking potatoes, scrubbed and cubed

2 garlic cloves, chopped

1 teaspoon ground black pepper

1. In a large pot, combine water, kale, potatoes, garlic, and black pepper.

2. Over high heat, bring soup to a boil, reduce heat to a simmer, and cover.

3. Allow soup to simmer for 30 minutes or until potatoes are fork-tender.

4. Remove from heat and allow to cool for 5 minutes.

5. Using an immersion blender, submerge blades and blend soup until all ingredients are well broken down and soup is fully blended, about 5 minutes.

6. Consume immediately or transfer soup to a large glass container with a tight-fitting lid. Soup can be stored in the refrigerator for up to 5 days or in the freezer for up to 1 month.

Per serving:

Calories: 113

Fat: 0.3 grams

Protein: 4.2 grams

Sodium: 45 milligrams

Carbohydrates: 25.4 grams

Sugar: 0.7 grams

Fiber: 2.6 grams

Blazing Broccoli

YIELDS 4 SERVINGS

8 cups purified water
4 cups broccoli florets
2 garlic cloves, chopped
1 tablespoon ground black pepper

1. In a large pot, combine water, broccoli, garlic, and black pepper.

2. Over high heat, bring soup to a boil, reduce heat to a simmer, and cover.

3. Allow soup to simmer for 15 minutes.

4. Using an immersion blender, submerge blades and blend soup until all ingredients are well broken down and soup is fully blended, about 5 minutes.

5. Remove from heat and allow to cool.

6. Consume immediately or transfer soup to a large glass container with a tight-fitting lid. Soup can be stored in the refrigerator for up to 5 days or in the freezer for up to 1 month.

Per serving:
Calories: 72
Fat: 0.6 grams
Protein: 7.2 grams
Sodium: 81 milligrams
Carbohydrates: 13.9 grams
Sugar: 0.0 grams
Fiber: 0.5 grams

Spicy Spinach and Garlic

YIELDS 4 SERVINGS

8 cups purified water

5 cups chopped spinach

4 garlic cloves, chopped

¼ teaspoon cayenne pepper

1. In a large pot, combine water, spinach, and garlic.

2. Over high heat, bring soup to a boil, reduce heat to a simmer, and cover.

3. Allow soup to simmer for 10–15 minutes.

4. Remove from heat and allow to cool for 5 minutes.

5. Add cayenne pepper. Using an immersion blender, submerge blades and blend soup until all ingredients are well broken down and soup is fully blended, about 5 minutes.

6. Consume immediately or transfer soup to a large glass container with a tight-fitting lid. Soup can be stored in the refrigerator for up to 5 days or in the freezer for up to 1 month.

Per serving:
Calories: 73
Fat: 0.72 grams
Protein: 8.5 grams

Sodium: 25 milligrams
Carbohydrates: 12.1 grams
Sugar: 1.3 grams
Fiber: 6.5 grams

Creamy Greens

YIELDS 4 SERVINGS

8 cups unsweetened almond milk

3 cups chopped spinach

1 cup chopped kale, ribs removed

1 cup chopped green cabbage

1 cup chopped green onions

1 garlic clove, chopped

1. In a large pot, combine all ingredients.

2. Over high heat, bring soup to a boil, reduce heat to a simmer, and cover.

3. Allow soup to simmer for 20 minutes or until vegetables are fork-tender.

4. Remove from heat and allow to cool for 5 minutes.

5. Using an immersion blender, submerge blades and blend soup until all ingredients are well broken down and soup is fully blended, about 5 minutes.

6. Consume immediately or transfer soup to a large glass container with a tight-fitting lid. Soup can be stored in the refrigerator for up to 5 days or in the freezer for up to 1 month.

ANTIOXIDANTS AND DETOXIFICATION

While the body moves through the transition of detox to a rejuvenated state of health, the potent antioxidants of whole, natural foods like fruits, vegetables, nuts, seeds, and flax can improve the nutritional value of your super soups immensely. By including a soup recipe like this one that packs a variety of antioxidant-rich greens in every sip of your soup, you can ensure your detoxifying capabilities remain as effective as possible. When you have plenty of antioxidants that help remove toxins, combat harmful cellular changes, and fight illness and disease, the result is a fully functioning synergistic system of immunity and optimal health that helps you achieve health goals simply and easily.

Per serving:
Calories: 120
Fat: 5.5 grams
Protein: 8.2 grams

Sodium: 469 milligrams
Carbohydrates: 10.9 grams
Sugar: 1.9 grams
Fiber: 5.2 grams

Sweet Peas, Greens, and Potatoes

YIELDS 4 SERVINGS

8 cups purified water

3 cups chopped spinach

1 cup chopped kale, ribs removed

2 baking potatoes, scrubbed and cubed

2 cups fresh sweet peas (may also use frozen and thawed)

1. In a large pot, combine water, spinach, kale, and potatoes.

2. Over high heat, bring soup to a boil, reduce heat to a simmer, and cover.

3. Allow soup to simmer for 30 minutes.

4. Add peas and simmer 5 minutes.

5. Remove from heat and allow to cool for 5 minutes.

6. Using an immersion blender, submerge blades and blend soup until all ingredients are well broken down and soup is fully blended, about 5 minutes.

7. Consume immediately or transfer soup to a large glass container with a tight-fitting lid. Soup can be stored in the refrigerator for up to 5 days or in the freezer for up to 1 month.

Per serving:
Calories: 224
Fat: 0.9 grams
Protein: 14.0 grams

Sodium: 172 milligrams
Carbohydrates: 43.8 grams
Sugar: 7.9 grams
Fiber: 11.4 grams

Cabbage-Vidalia-Spinach

YIELDS 4 SERVINGS

8 cups purified water

1 cup chopped green cabbage

2 cups chopped Vidalia onions

2 garlic cloves, chopped

6 cups spinach

1. In a large pot, combine water, cabbage, onion, and garlic.

2. Over high heat, bring soup to a boil, reduce heat to a simmer, and cover.

3. Allow soup to simmer for 30 minutes.

4. Add spinach, stirring for 5 minutes or until spinach is wilted.

5. Remove from heat and allow to cool for 5 minutes.

6. Using an immersion blender, submerge blades and blend soup until all ingredients are well broken down and soup is fully blended, about 5 minutes.

7. Consume immediately or transfer soup to a large glass container with a tight-fitting lid. Soup can be stored in the refrigerator for up to 5 days or in the freezer for up to 1 month.

Per serving:
Calories: 113
Fat: 0.8 grams
Protein: 10.9 grams

Sodium: 30 milligrams
Carbohydrates: 22.6 grams
Sugar: 6.2 grams
Fiber: 8.9 grams

Split Pea

YIELDS 4 SERVINGS

2 tablespoons extra-virgin olive oil

1 yellow onion, peeled and chopped

1 cup chopped celery

1 (16-ounce) bag split peas

1 tablespoon ground marjoram

½ tablespoon salt

8 cups Simple Vegetable-Based Poultry Broth (see Chapter 10)

1. In a large pot over high heat, combine the olive oil, onion, celery, split peas, marjoram, and salt. Sauté until vegetables are slightly tender, about 5 minutes.

2. Add stock to the pot and bring soup to a boil. Reduce heat to a simmer and cover.

3. Allow soup to simmer for 1 hour or until vegetables are fork-tender.

4. Remove from heat and allow to cool.

5. Using an immersion blender, submerge blades and blend soup until ingredients are well blended and desired consistency is achieved, about 5 minutes.

6. Consume immediately or transfer soup to a large glass container with a tight-fitting lid and store in the refrigerator for up to 5 days.

Per serving:
Calories: 534
Fat: 9.2 grams
Protein: 30.8 grams

Sodium: 971 milligrams
Carbohydrates: 84.1 grams
Sugar: 16.0 grams
Fiber: 30.7 grams

Healthy Guacamole Soup

YIELDS 3 SERVINGS

4 cups purified water

¼ cup lime juice

2 Hass avocados, peeled and seeded

1 garlic clove, chopped

2 Roma tomatoes, chopped

½ cup chopped red onions

½ cup chopped celery

1 teaspoon salt

1 teaspoon ground black pepper

1. In a blender, combine water, lime juice, avocados, and garlic.

2. Blend on high until desired consistency is achieved, about 2 minutes.

3. Transfer avocado soup to a large glass container and add the chopped tomatoes, onion, and celery. Add salt and pepper and stir to combine ingredients thoroughly.

4. Consume immediately or transfer soup to a large glass container with a tight-fitting lid. Soup can be stored in the refrigerator for about 1 day without changing color to a brownish hue. Once the soup has changed color, discard.

Per serving:

Calories: 202

Fat: 13.2 grams

Protein: 3.2 grams

Sodium: 815 milligrams

Carbohydrates: 19.7 grams

Sugar: 7.6 grams

Fiber: 7.9 grams

Avocado Mint

YIELDS 4 SERVINGS

8 cups purified water

2 Hass avocados, peeled and seeded

2 large cucumbers, scrubbed and peeled with ends removed

2 cups chopped fresh mint leaves

1 garlic clove

1 teaspoon ground black pepper

1. In a countertop blender, combine all ingredients.

2. Blend on high until ingredients are well blended and desired consistency is achieved, about 5 minutes.

3. Consume immediately or transfer soup to a large glass container with a tight-fitting lid. Soup can be stored in the refrigerator for up to 5 days or in the freezer for up to 1 month.

Per serving:

Calories: 141

Fat: 9.5 grams

Protein: 2.7 grams

Sodium: 30 milligrams

Carbohydrates: 11.4 grams

Sugar: 2.2 grams

Fiber: 6.8 grams

Spicy Citrus and Greens

YIELDS 4 SERVINGS

6 cups purified water

1 cup freshly squeezed orange juice

1 pink grapefruit, peeled and seeded

6 cups chopped spinach

1 tablespoon grated ginger

1. In a countertop blender, combine all ingredients.

2. Blend on high until ingredients are broken down and thoroughly combined, about 2 minutes.

3. Consume immediately or transfer soup to a large glass container with a tight-fitting lid. Soup can be stored in the refrigerator for up to 5 days or in the freezer for up to 1 month.

Per serving:

Calories: 127

Fat: 1.0 grams

Protein: 10.7 grams

Sodium: 29 milligrams

Carbohydrates: 24.1 grams

Sugar: 7.7 grams

Fiber: 8.5 grams

Sweet Green Pea Soup

YIELDS 4 SERVINGS

8 cups purified water

3 cups fresh sweet peas (may also use frozen and thawed)

1 cup chopped spinach

1. In a blender, combine all ingredients.

2. Blend on high until ingredients are broken down and thoroughly combined, about 3 minutes.

3. Consume immediately or transfer soup to a large glass container with a tight-fitting lid. Soup can be stored in the refrigerator for up to 5 days or in the freezer for up to 1 month.

DELICIOUS DETOX

Some people dread the detoxification process, assuming that the normal cleanse and detox involves restriction, starvation, and lack of energy. But with a cleanse like the soup cleanse that involves regular servings of amazingly healthy soups every three hours that can be eaten in whatever amount necessary to reach the desired feeling of fullness, you can make detoxing easy and delicious with benefits like immunity-boosting antioxidants and detoxifying vitamins, minerals, and phytochemicals that combine to boost health in every way!

Per serving:
Calories: 89
Fat: 0.3 grams
Protein: 6.1 grams

Sodium: 48 milligrams
Carbohydrates: 16 grams
Sugar: 6.2 grams
Fiber: 5.7 grams

Green Thai Soup

4 cups purified water

4 cups unsweetened coconut milk

½ cup lime juice

2 tablespoons green curry paste

1 cup chopped Vidalia onions

1 cup chopped green onions

2 cups chopped spinach

2 garlic cloves, chopped

¼ cup chopped lemongrass

1. In a large pot, combine all ingredients.

2. Over high heat, bring soup to a boil, reduce heat to a simmer, and cover.

3. Allow soup to simmer for 15 minutes or until onion and lemongrass are fork-tender.

4. Remove from heat and allow to cool for 5 minutes.

5. Using an immersion blender, submerge blades and blend soup until all ingredients are well broken down and soup is fully blended, about 5 minutes.

6. Consume immediately or transfer soup to a large glass container with a tight-fitting lid. Soup can be stored in the refrigerator for up to 5 days or in the freezer for up to 1 month.

Per serving:
Calories: 121
Fat: 4.4 grams
Protein: 4.5 grams

Sodium: 306 milligrams
Carbohydrates: 16.7 grams
Sugar: 4.4 grams
Fiber: 4.0 grams

Garlicky Green Trio

YIELDS 4 SERVINGS

8 cups purified water

2 cups chopped kale, ribs removed

2 cups chopped green cabbage

4 garlic cloves, chopped

4 cups chopped spinach

1. In a large pot, combine water, kale, cabbage, and garlic.

2. Over high heat, bring soup to a boil, reduce heat to a simmer, and cover.

3. Allow soup to simmer for 20–25 minutes or until kale and cabbage are fork-tender.

4. Add spinach and stir constantly until spinach is wilted, about 5 minutes.

5. Remove from heat and allow to cool for 5 minutes.

6. Using an immersion blender, submerge blades and blend soup until all ingredients are well broken down and soup is fully blended, about 5 minutes.

7. Consume immediately or transfer soup to a large glass container with a tight-fitting lid. Soup can be stored in the refrigerator for up to 5 days or in the freezer for up to 1 month.

Per serving:
Calories: 87
Fat: 0.8 grams
Protein: 8.6 grams

Sodium: 47 milligrams
Carbohydrates: 15.9 grams
Sugar: 2.44 grams
Fiber: 6.9 grams

Minty Sweet Pea

YIELDS 4 SERVINGS

8 cups purified water

3 cups fresh sweet peas (may also use frozen and thawed)

2 cups chopped fresh mint leaves

1. In a large pot, combine water and peas.

2. Over high heat, bring soup to a boil, reduce heat to a simmer, and cover.

3. Allow soup to simmer for 10 minutes.

4. Add mint and continue to simmer for 2–5 minutes.

5. Remove from heat and allow to cool for 5 minutes.

6. Using an immersion blender, submerge blades and blend soup until all ingredients are well broken down and soup is fully blended, about 5 minutes.

7. Consume immediately or transfer soup to a large glass container with a tight-fitting lid. Soup can be stored in the refrigerator for up to 5 days or in the freezer for up to 1 month.

Per serving:
Calories: 96
Fat: 0.4 grams
Protein: 6.4 grams

Sodium: 72 milligrams
Carbohydrates: 17.6 grams
Sugar: 6.2 grams
Fiber: 6.6 grams

CHAPTER 5

Energy-Boosting Soups

To enjoy a day with ample amounts of energy is a reality some people only dream of. With the right combination of nutrient-dense foods that optimize the processes of the body that create energy, though, this dream can be your reality! The ingredients in this chapter's recipes, like warm spices, omega-rich nuts and flax, nutrient-dense fruits and vegetables, and protein-rich additions, all work to boost energy, improve metabolism, and support the body in storing and utilizing carbohydrates, fats, and proteins for energy. They can all also help you create a new life of energy and endurance, focus and clarity, and give you the ability to wake up feeling refreshed and energized!

Because nutrients are readily available through each and every meal, the body is able to function at its best without having to slow down to conserve energy. The result can be a major transformation. Vitamins like A, Bs, C, and E, in combination with iron, calcium, magnesium, and potent phytochemicals that help protect cell health and promote optimal functioning of the body's brain and systems, are packed into every one of these delicious and nutritious recipes. With soups like Cinnamon-Almond with Flax, Ginger-Citrus Cream, Creamy Kiwi Pineapple, and Creamy Cashew Squash with Flax, this chapter focuses on clean, energy-boosting ingredients that not only help you achieve your health goals but give you energy to burn while doing it!

Carrot-Almond with Cardamom

YIELDS 4 SERVINGS

8 cups purified water

2 cups raw almonds

8 carrots, ends removed, peeled, and chopped

1 tablespoon cardamom

1. In a large pot, combine all ingredients.

2. Over high heat, bring soup to a boil, reduce heat to a simmer, and cover.

3. Allow soup to simmer for 1 hour or until almonds are tender.

4. Remove from heat and allow to cool for 5 minutes.

5. Using an immersion blender, submerge blades and blend until all ingredients are broken down and thoroughly blended and desired consistency is achieved, about 5 minutes.

6. Consume immediately or transfer soup to a large glass container with a tight-fitting lid. Soup can be stored in the refrigerator for up to 5 days or in the freezer for up to 1 month.

Per serving:
Calories: 467
Fat: 36.4 grams
Protein: 16.5 grams

Sodium: 103 milligrams
Carbohydrates: 26.8 grams
Sugar: 9.2 grams
Fiber: 12.3 grams

Citrus Asparagus Cream

YIELDS 4 SERVINGS

8 cups unsweetened almond milk

6 cups asparagus spears

1 cup freshly squeezed lime juice

1. In a large pot, combine almond milk and asparagus.

2. Over high heat, bring soup to a boil, reduce heat to a simmer, and cover.

3. Allow soup to simmer for 15 minutes or until asparagus spears are fork-tender.

4. Remove from heat, add lime juice, and allow to cool for 5 minutes.

5. Using an immersion blender, submerge blades and blend until all ingredients are broken down and thoroughly blended and desired consistency is achieved, about 5 minutes.

6. Consume immediately or transfer soup to a large glass container with a tight-fitting lid. Soup can be stored in the refrigerator for up to 5 days or in the freezer for up to 1 month.

B VITAMINS BOOST ENERGY NATURALLY

With the soup cleanse's natural ingredients like citrus fruits, green vegetables like asparagus, and healthy additions like almond milk, soups pack a ton of B vitamins into every single sip. If the goal of your cleanse is to have more energy, these B vitamins are the best! Helping to improve hormone levels, particularly serotonin and dopamine that are required for energy and focus, B vitamins help you eat for higher energy levels that last throughout the day!

Per serving:
Calories: 114
Fat: 5.2 grams
Protein: 6.7 grams

Sodium: 325 milligrams
Carbohydrates: 12.6 grams
Sugar: 4.8 grams
Fiber: 4.6 grams

Creamy Figs and Grains

YIELDS 4 SERVINGS

8 cups unsweetened vanilla almond milk

8 figs, stems removed and skin intact

1 cup organic apple juice (not from concentrate)

2 cups cooked quinoa

1. In a large pot, combine almond milk and figs.

2. Over high heat, bring soup to a boil, reduce heat to a simmer, and cover.

3. Allow soup to simmer for 20 minutes or until figs are softened.

4. Remove from heat, add apple juice, and allow to cool for 5 minutes.

5. Using an immersion blender, submerge blades and blend until all ingredients are broken down and thoroughly blended and desired consistency is achieved, about 5 minutes.

6. Stir in cooked quinoa until well blended.

7. Consume immediately or transfer soup to a large glass container with a tight-fitting lid. Soup can be stored in the refrigerator for up to 5 days or in the freezer for up to 1 month.

Per serving:
Calories: 268
Fat: 5.2 grams
Protein: 7.7 grams

Sodium: 331 milligrams
Carbohydrates: 42.2 grams
Sugar: 14.0 grams
Fiber: 5.0 grams

Three-Berry Spiced Soup

YIELDS 4 SERVINGS

8 cups organic apple juice (not from concentrate)

2 cups strawberries, tops removed

2 cups blueberries

2 cups raspberries

1 tablespoon ground cardamom

1 teaspoon ground cloves

2" piece of ginger, peeled and sliced

1. In a countertop blender, combine all ingredients.

2. Blend on high until all ingredients are broken down and thoroughly combined, about 2–3 minutes.

3. Consume immediately or transfer soup to a large glass container with a tight-fitting lid. Soup can be stored in the refrigerator for up to 5 days or in the freezer for up to 1 month.

VITAMIN C FOR ENERGY IMPROVEMENTS

When the immune system works as intended, the body experiences fewer bouts of illness and disease, which are arguably the most energy-draining situations that you can face. With the immune system functioning at its best and keeping illnesses at bay, the body is able to absorb the energy-boosting nutrients of foods better, helping energy levels soar naturally! Vitamin C–rich fruits, vegetables, and spices (like ginger!) all contribute to the protection of the immune system, supporting energy production that can remain high throughout the day.

Per serving:
Calories: 386
Fat: 1.4 grams
Protein: 3.5 grams

Sodium: 24 milligrams
Carbohydrates: 94.3 grams
Sugar: 67.9 grams
Fiber: 13.4 grams

Spiced Nut Milk Soup

YIELDS 4 SERVINGS

8 cups unsweetened vanilla almond milk

2 cups raw almonds

2 cups raw cashews

2 cups walnuts

¼ cup ground flaxseed

1 tablespoon ground nutmeg

1 tablespoon ground cinnamon

1 teaspoon ground cloves

1" piece of ginger, peeled and sliced

1 tablespoon maple syrup

1. In a large pot, combine all ingredients.

2. Over high heat, bring soup to a boil, reduce heat to a simmer, and cover.

3. Allow soup to simmer for 40–60 minutes or until nuts are soft.

4. Remove from heat and allow to cool for 5 minutes.

5. Using an immersion blender, submerge blades and blend until all ingredients are broken down and thoroughly blended and desired consistency is achieved, about 5 minutes.

6. Consume immediately or transfer soup to a large glass container with a tight-fitting lid. Soup can be stored in the refrigerator for up to 5 days or in the freezer for up to 1 month.

Per serving:
Calories: 1702
Fat: 149.4 grams
Protein: 49.7 grams

Sodium: 335 milligrams
Carbohydrates: 60.2 grams
Sugar: 13.7 grams
Fiber: 22.3 grams

Thai Cabbage Soup

YIELDS 4 SERVINGS

8 cups unsweetened coconut milk

4 cups chopped green cabbage

1 red onion, peeled and chopped

1 red bell pepper, seeded and chopped

1 cup chopped lemongrass

1 tablespoon red curry paste

½ teaspoon cayenne pepper

1. In a large pot, combine all ingredients.

2. Over high heat, bring soup to a boil, reduce heat to a simmer, and cover.

3. Allow soup to simmer for 30–40 minutes or until all vegetables are fork-tender.

4. Remove from heat and allow to cool.

5. Consume immediately or transfer soup to a large glass container with a tight-fitting lid. Soup can be stored in the refrigerator for up to 5 days or in the freezer for up to 1 month.

Per serving:

Calories: 196

Fat: 8.4 grams

Protein: 2.9 grams

Sodium: 216 milligrams

Carbohydrates: 25.9 grams

Sugar: 5.7 grams

Fiber: 3.6 grams

Creamy Coconut Citrus

YIELDS 4 SERVINGS

8 cups coconut milk

2 oranges, peeled and seeded

1 pink grapefruit, peeled and seeded

2 cups chopped pineapple

2 kiwis, peeled and halved

½ cup lime juice

1. In a countertop blender, combine all ingredients.

2. Blend on high until all ingredients are broken down and thoroughly combined, about 2–3 minutes.

3. Consume immediately or transfer soup to a large glass container with a tight-fitting lid. Soup can be stored in the refrigerator for up to 5 days or in the freezer for up to 1 month.

Per serving:

Calories: 284

Fat: 10.3 grams

Protein: 1.8 grams

Sodium: 72 milligrams

Carbohydrates: 46.5 grams

Sugar: 39.2 grams

Fiber: 5.4 grams

Ginger-Citrus Cream

YIELDS 4 SERVINGS

6 cups unsweetened vanilla almond milk

2 cups Greek yogurt

2 oranges, peeled and seeded

1 grapefruit, peeled and seeded

2 cups chopped pineapple

1" piece of ginger, peeled and chopped

1. In a countertop blender, combine all ingredients.

2. Blend on high until all ingredients are broken down and well blended.

3. Consume immediately or transfer soup to a large glass container with a tight-fitting lid and store in the refrigerator for up to 5 days.

Per serving:
Calories: 259
Fat: 9.0 grams
Protein: 12.2 grams

Sodium: 276 milligrams
Carbohydrates: 34.9 grams
Sugar: 26.5 grams
Fiber: 4.5 grams

Chai Nut Milk with Pineapple

YIELDS 4 SERVINGS

8 cups vanilla almond milk

2 cups raw almonds

2 cups raw cashews

4 tablespoons ground cardamom

2 cups chopped pineapple

1. In a countertop blender, combine almond milk, almonds, cashews, and cardamom.

2. Blend on high until nuts are broken down and thoroughly blended, about 1 minute.

3. Add pineapple and blend on high until all ingredients are well combined, about 1 minute.

4. Consume immediately or transfer soup to a large glass container with a tight-fitting lid. Soup can be stored in the refrigerator for up to 5 days or in the freezer for up to 1 month.

Per serving:
Calories: 1082
Fat: 74.4 grams
Protein: 32.1 grams

Sodium: 331 milligrams
Carbohydrates: 87.9 grams
Sugar: 51.2 grams
Fiber: 14.2 grams

Cool Cream of Asparagus

YIELDS 4 SERVINGS

6 cups unsweetened almond milk

2 cups Greek yogurt

4 cups cooked and cooled asparagus spears

1 cucumber, peeled and chopped

1 Hass avocado, peeled and seeded

1. In a countertop blender, combine all ingredients.

2. Blend on high until all ingredients are broken down and thoroughly blended and desired consistency is achieved, about 2–3 minutes.

3. Consume immediately or transfer soup to a large glass container with a tight-fitting lid. Soup can be stored in the refrigerator for up to 5 days or in the freezer for up to 1 month.

CLEAN-EATING BENEFITS

The focus on clean-eating benefits is nothing new to the world of nutrition, but the message is being accepted by more and more people, including physicians, holistic healers, and average people around the world. There is no easier way to eat clean than by consuming a diet focused on whole foods just like those found in this recipe; asparagus, cucumbers, and avocados make for nutrient-dense additions to any soup cleanse routine, providing the body with wholesome whole-food goodness that's not only nutritious but delicious, too!

Per serving:
Calories: 229
Fat: 13.6 grams
Protein: 14.4 grams

Sodium: 281 milligrams
Carbohydrates: 13.2 grams
Sugar: 7.3 grams
Fiber: 5.5 grams

Apple Cider Vinegar–Spiked Avocado Cream

YIELDS 4 SERVINGS

6 cups unsweetened almond milk

1 cup Greek yogurt

4 Hass avocados, peeled and seeded

2 tablespoons apple cider vinegar

1" piece of ginger, peeled and sliced

1. In a countertop blender, combine all ingredients.

2. Blend on high until all ingredients are broken down and thoroughly blended and desired consistency is achieved, about 2–3 minutes.

3. Consume immediately or transfer soup to a large glass container with a tight-fitting lid. Soup can be stored in the refrigerator for up to 5 days or in the freezer for up to 1 month.

FOODS FOR FOCUS

When your brain feels overwhelmed, tired, or "fuzzy," it's harder than ever to keep your energy levels up. Fortunately, with a diet of natural, whole foods like this recipe's avocados and ginger that provide the brain and body with plentiful vitamins, minerals, and phytochemicals that deliver the essential nutrients the brain and body need (without the toxins that wreak havoc on the body's systems), you'll find yourself enjoying higher energy levels and better focus that result in more productive, happier, healthier, and fulfilling days.

Per serving:
Calories: 325
Fat: 25.0 grams
Protein: 8.8 grams

Sodium: 269 milligrams
Carbohydrates: 14.9 grams
Sugar: 2.5 grams
Fiber: 9.4 grams

Creamy Kiwi Pineapple

YIELDS 4 SERVINGS

6 cups coconut milk

2 cups Greek yogurt

4 kiwis, peeled and halved

3 cups chopped pineapple

1. In a countertop blender, combine all ingredients.

2. Blend on high until all ingredients are broken down and thoroughly blended and desired consistency is achieved, about 2–3 minutes.

3. Consume immediately or transfer soup to a large glass container with a tight-fitting lid. Soup can be stored in the refrigerator for up to 5 days or in the freezer for up to 1 month.

NUTRITION: THE NATURAL REMEDY FOR FATIGUE

With the overwhelming amounts of sugar, sodium, preservatives, and unhealthy fats in the average person's diet, the most common complaint among people is fatigue. Why? These elements drain the body of energy by overwhelming it with spiking and plummeting blood-sugar levels, hard-to-process preservatives and fats, and sodium-induced water retention and bloating that all combine to zap energy and create fatigue. Getting up and moving in the morning, maintaining steady energy levels, and falling asleep at night become easier with a diet focused on whole foods like the protein-rich Greek yogurt and vitamin C–rich pineapple and kiwi in this recipe that keep energy-regulating hormones, blood-sugar levels, and every system functioning properly and at its best.

Per serving:
Calories: 312
Fat: 12.8 grams
Protein: 10.3 grams

Sodium: 90 milligrams
Carbohydrates: 39.2 grams
Sugar: 31.9 grams
Fiber: 3.5 grams

Spiced Creamy Figs

YIELDS 4 SERVINGS

8 cups vanilla almond milk

8 figs, stems removed and skins intact

2" piece of ginger, peeled and chopped

2 tablespoons ground cinnamon

1 tablespoon ground cardamom

2 teaspoons ground cloves

1. In a large pot, combine the almond milk, figs, and ginger; season with the cinnamon, cardamom, and cloves.

2. Over high heat, bring soup to a boil, reduce heat to a simmer, and cover.

3. Allow soup to simmer for 25–30 minutes.

4. Remove from heat and allow to cool for 5 minutes.

5. Using an immersion blender, submerge blades and blend on high until figs and ginger are broken down and the soup is well blended, about 5 minutes.

6. Consume immediately or transfer soup to a large glass container with a tight-fitting lid. Soup can be stored in the refrigerator for up to 5 days or in the freezer for up to 1 month.

Per serving:
Calories: 260
Fat: 5.5 grams
Protein: 3.1 grams

Sodium: 324 milligrams
Carbohydrates: 53.2 grams
Sugar: 45.2 grams
Fiber: 5.3 grams

Fruity Fig Chai Cream

YIELDS 4 SERVINGS

6 cups vanilla almond milk

2 cups Greek yogurt

4 figs, stems removed

2 cups chopped pineapple

1 peach, pit removed

4 tablespoons ground cardamom

1. In a countertop blender, combine all ingredients.

2. Blend on high until all ingredients are broken down and thoroughly blended and desired consistency is achieved, about 2–3 minutes.

3. Consume immediately or transfer soup to a large glass container with a tight-fitting lid. Soup can be stored in the refrigerator for up to 5 days or in the freezer for up to 1 month.

Per serving:	
Calories: 340	Sodium: 277 milligrams
Fat: 9.1 grams	Carbohydrates: 55.8 grams
Protein: 12.4 grams	Sugar: 47.3 grams
	Fiber: 4.8 grams

Melon Trio Cooler

YIELDS 4 SERVINGS

2 cups vanilla almond milk

2 cups Greek yogurt

4 cups chopped watermelon

4 cups chopped cantaloupe

4 cups chopped honeydew

1. In a countertop blender, combine all ingredients.

2. Blend on high until all ingredients are broken down and thoroughly blended and desired consistency is achieved, about 2–3 minutes.

3. Consume immediately or transfer soup to a large glass container with a tight-fitting lid. Soup can be stored in the refrigerator for up to 5 days or in the freezer for up to 1 month.

Per serving:	
Calories: 326	Sodium: 173 milligrams
Fat: 6.9 grams	Carbohydrates: 58.4 grams
Protein: 13.2 grams	Sugar: 53.1 grams
	Fiber: 3.8 grams

Almond-Cashew Cream with Quinoa and Flax

YIELDS 4 SERVINGS

8 cups vanilla almond milk

2 cups raw almonds

2 cups raw cashews

¼ cup ground flaxseed

2 cups cooked quinoa

1. In a countertop blender, combine the almond milk, almonds, cashews, and flaxseed.

2. Blend on high until all ingredients are broken down and thoroughly blended and desired consistency is achieved, about 2–3 minutes.

3. Add quinoa and stir until all ingredients are well combined.

4. Consume immediately or transfer soup to a large glass container with a tight-fitting lid. Soup can be stored in the refrigerator for up to 5 days or in the freezer for up to 1 month.

Per serving:
Calories: 1181
Fat: 77.2 grams
Protein: 37.0 grams

Sodium: 339 milligrams
Carbohydrates: 95.3 grams
Sugar: 39.9 grams
Fiber: 16.2 grams

Quinoa Berry Blend with Leafy Greens

YIELDS 4 SERVINGS

8 cups unsweetened vanilla almond milk

2 cups strawberries, tops removed

2 cups blueberries

1 cup chopped spinach

2 cups cooked quinoa

1. In a countertop blender, combine almond milk, strawberries, blueberries, and spinach.

2. Blend on high until all ingredients are broken down and thoroughly blended and desired consistency is achieved, about 2–3 minutes.

3. Add quinoa and stir until all ingredients are well blended.

4. Consume immediately or transfer soup to a large glass container with a tight-fitting lid. Soup can be stored in the refrigerator for up to 5 days or in the freezer for up to 1 month.

Per serving:
Calories: 299
Fat: 5.5 grams
Protein: 10.0 grams

Sodium: 374 milligrams
Carbohydrates: 48.8 grams
Sugar: 15.2 grams
Fiber: 8.7 grams

CHAPTER 6

Weight-Loss Soups

Whether you need to lose five pounds or fifty, the most effective way to lose weight healthfully is to focus on nutrition. With the quality nutrition found in the soups in this chapter, you can increase energy levels, maximize metabolic functioning, fight cravings, and support your body's systems that play major roles in the process of fat loss and muscle gain, all intricate parts of the successful, sustained weight-loss process. With the fiber-filled vibrant vegetables and sweet fruits, along with the protein-rich additions like almond milk, nuts, and seeds, the delightful nutritious and delicious recipes in this chapter make for filling meals and snacks that pack nutrient-dense ingredients that help increase energy, speed up metabolism, and curb cravings for easy weight loss.

These nutrients also help stoke your metabolic fire, keeping your energy level up and helping you begin and maintain an active lifestyle. The best part of increasing your energy and metabolic processes through quality, fiber-filled, fat-burning ingredients like those found in the recipes of this chapter is that you'll find yourself able to enjoy physical activity with a newfound endurance that only improves your weight-loss efforts and increases your chances of success! With delicious recipes like Miso Vegetable, Fajita Quinoa, Tomato-Basil Tofu, and Ginger-Carrot Bisque, you can savor the flavors of sweet and savory soups that keep you feeling satisfied while satisfying your body's needs for nutrition that promote the fat-loss and energy needs anyone wanting to lose weight needs!

Cabbage Soup

YIELDS 4 SERVINGS

8 cups purified water

6 cups chopped green cabbage

½ cup apple cider vinegar

1. In a large pot, combine water and cabbage.

2. Over high heat, bring soup to a boil, reduce heat to a simmer, and cover.

3. Allow soup to simmer for 20–30 minutes or until cabbage is fork-tender.

4. Remove from heat and allow to cool for 1 hour.

5. Add apple cider vinegar, stirring well to combine thoroughly.

6. Consume immediately or transfer soup to a large glass container with a tight-fitting lid. Soup can be stored in the refrigerator for up to 5 days or in the freezer for up to 1 month.

Per serving:
Calories: 39
Fat: 0.1 grams
Protein: 1.7 grams
Sodium: 26 milligrams
Carbohydrates: 8.0 grams
Sugar: 4.4 grams
Fiber: 3.3 grams

Lemon-Ginger Tofu Soup with Noodles

YIELDS 4 SERVINGS

6 cups purified water

2 cups freshly squeezed lemon juice

2" piece of ginger, peeled and sliced

1 (16-ounce) package firm tofu, cubed into ¼" pieces

1 (16-ounce) package rice noodles

1. In a large pot, combine water, lemon juice, ginger, and tofu.

2. Over high heat, bring soup to a boil, reduce heat to a simmer, and cover.

3. Allow soup to simmer for 20–30 minutes.

4. Add rice noodles and stir for 5 minutes or until noodles are softened.

5. Remove from heat and allow to cool.

6. Consume immediately or transfer soup to a large glass container with a tight-fitting lid. Soup can be stored in the refrigerator for up to 5 days or in the freezer for up to 1 month.

LEMONS FOR IMPROVED METABOLIC FUNCTIONING

Starring in cleanses and detoxes for hundreds of years, lemons have long been used for the purpose of restoring health. With ample amounts of vitamin C, fiber, and an assortment of unique phytochemicals, lemons also possess natural enzymes that can improve each and every system throughout the body, helping to support the metabolic process and all of the systems like digestion, nervous-system functioning, immunity, and even mental functioning.

Per serving:

Calories: 524

Fat: 6.1 grams

Protein: 16.6 grams

Sodium: 63 milligrams

Carbohydrates: 101.5 grams

Sugar: 3.5 grams

Fiber: 1.3 grams

Miso Vegetable

YIELDS 4 SERVINGS

8 cups plus 2 tablespoons purified water

2 cups chopped green cabbage

2 cups chopped red onions

2 cups chopped spinach

2 tablespoons white miso paste

1. In a large pot, combine 8 cups water, cabbage, and red onion.

2. Over high heat, bring soup to a boil, reduce heat to a simmer, and cover.

3. Allow soup to simmer for 20 minutes or until vegetables are tender.

4. Stir in spinach, allow to wilt for 5 minutes.

5. In a small dish, whisk together the miso paste and remaining 2 tablespoons water until well blended. Add to soup and stir to combine thoroughly.

6. Remove from heat and allow to cool.

7. Consume immediately or transfer soup to a large glass container with a tight-fitting lid. Soup can be stored in the refrigerator for up to 5 days or in the freezer for up to 1 month.

Per serving:
Calories: 87
Fat: 1.0 grams
Protein: 5.8 grams

Sodium: 493 milligrams
Carbohydrates: 16.4 grams
Sugar: 5.7 grams
Fiber: 5.5 grams

Curried Carrot and Cabbage

YIELDS 4 SERVINGS

8 cups purified water

4 cups chopped red cabbage

4 cups peeled and chopped carrots

4 tablespoons curry powder

1 tablespoon garlic powder

1. In a large pot, combine water, cabbage, and carrots.

2. Over high heat, bring soup to a boil, reduce heat to a simmer, and cover.

3. Allow soup to simmer for 30 minutes or until carrots are tender.

4. Remove from heat and allow to cool for 5 minutes.

5. Add curry and garlic. Using an immersion blender, submerge blades and blend on high until all ingredients are broken down and thoroughly combined, about 5 minutes.

6. Consume immediately or transfer soup to a large glass container with a tight-fitting lid. Soup can be stored in the refrigerator for up to 5 days or in the freezer for up to 1 month.

CURRY'S WARMTH

Packed with essential metabolism-boosting nutrients, curry provides the body with ample amounts of energy-boosting B vitamins and enough calcium and magnesium to support the functioning of the body's digestion, absorption, and processing of every nutrient the body requires to function optimally. Delicious and nutritious, curry is the spice of life that promotes health and well-being, and it also helps speed metabolic functioning and supports weight loss and muscle gain.

Per serving:
Calories: 120
Fat: 1.0 grams
Protein: 4.2 grams

Sodium: 146 milligrams
Carbohydrates: 27.1 grams
Sugar: 11.2 grams
Fiber: 8.6 grams

Cabbage, Leek, and Carrots with Ginger

YIELDS 4 SERVINGS

8 cups purified water

4 cups chopped cabbage

2 cups chopped leeks

2 carrots, peeled and sliced

2" piece of ginger, peeled and minced

1. In a large pot, combine all ingredients.

2. Over high heat, bring soup to a boil, reduce heat to a simmer, and cover.

3. Allow soup to simmer for 30–45 minutes or until all vegetables are tender.

4. Remove from heat and allow to cool.

5. Consume immediately or transfer soup to a large glass container with a tight-fitting lid. Soup can be stored in the refrigerator for up to 5 days or in the freezer for up to 1 month.

Per serving:

Calories: 64

Fat: 0.2 grams

Protein: 2.1 grams

Sodium: 64 milligrams

Carbohydrates: 14.9 grams

Sugar: 6.1 grams

Fiber: 3.9 grams

Bell-Pepper Trio

YIELDS 4 SERVINGS

8 cups purified water

2 cups sliced red bell peppers

2 cups sliced yellow bell peppers

2 cups sliced green bell peppers

4 tablespoons ground cumin

2 tablespoons garlic powder

1. In a large pot, combine all ingredients.

2. Over high heat, bring soup to a boil, reduce heat to a simmer, and cover.

3. Allow soup to simmer for 30 minutes or until peppers are softened and soup is fragrant.

4. Remove from heat and allow to cool.

5. Consume immediately or transfer soup to a large glass container with a tight-fitting lid. Soup can be stored in the refrigerator for up to 5 days or in the freezer for up to 1 month.

Per serving:

Calories: 74

Fat: 1.3 grams

Protein: 3.2 grams

Sodium: 35 milligrams

Carbohydrates: 14.0 grams

Sugar: 3.3 grams

Fiber: 3.2 grams

Citrus, Cabbage, and Spinach with Apple Cider Vinegar and Aloe

YIELDS 4 SERVINGS

8 cups purified water

4 cups chopped green cabbage

4 cups spinach

¼ cup lemon juice

⅛ cup apple cider vinegar

⅛ cup aloe vera juice

1. In a large pot, combine water and cabbage.

2. Over high heat, bring soup to a boil, reduce heat to a simmer, and cover.

3. Allow soup to simmer for 20 minutes or until cabbage is tender.

4. Add spinach, stirring until leaves are wilted, about 1–2 minutes.

5. Remove from heat and allow to cool for 5 minutes. Add lemon juice, apple cider vinegar, and aloe vera juice and stir to combine well.

6. Consume immediately or transfer soup to a large glass container with a tight-fitting lid. Soup can be stored in the refrigerator for up to 5 days or in the freezer for up to 1 month.

APPLE CIDER VINEGAR FOR WEIGHT LOSS

With its potent, naturally occurring enzymes (referred to as "the mother") unique to the organic unfiltered varieties of apple cider vinegar, this healthful addition makes the perfect weight-loss-supporting ingredient in your favorite savory soups. Promoting the health of the circulatory system, muscle growth, and the breakdown of fat, apple cider vinegar helps support every aspect of the body's weight-loss process to ensure your weight-loss efforts are successful and your health goals are achieved.

Per serving:
Calories: 83
Fat: 0.6 grams
Protein: 7.8 grams

Sodium: 41 milligrams
Carbohydrates: 15.6 grams
Sugar: 5.0 grams
Fiber: 7.3 grams

Ginger-Carrot Bisque

YIELDS 4 SERVINGS

8 cups unsweetened vanilla almond milk
6 cups peeled and chopped carrots
4" piece of ginger, peeled and chopped
1 teaspoon ground cloves

1. In a large pot, combine almond milk, carrots, and ginger; season with cloves.

2. Over high heat, bring soup to a boil, reduce heat to a simmer, and cover.

3. Allow soup to simmer for 30 minutes or until carrots and ginger are tender.

4. Remove from heat and allow to cool for 5 minutes.

5. Using an immersion blender, submerge blades in soup and blend on high until all ingredients are broken down and thoroughly combined, about 5 minutes.

6. Consume immediately or transfer soup to a large glass container with a tight-fitting lid. Soup can be stored in the refrigerator for up to 5 days or in the freezer for up to 1 month.

GINGER'S POTENT COMPOUNDS

Ginger has been used as a medicinal herb for over 2,000 years. Gingerol and shogaol, the dehydrated form of gingerol, are compounds that contribute to countless functions throughout the body, especially those that facilitate weight loss. Helping the bones and muscles absorb and process essential nutrients from the foods we eat, ginger helps improve energy levels, increase muscle strength, and fight fat accumulation throughout the body.

Per serving:
Calories: 149
Fat: 5.5 grams
Protein: 4.0 grams

Sodium: 455 milligrams
Carbohydrates: 20.8 grams
Sugar: 9.3 grams
Fiber: 5.8 grams

Onion-Mushroom with Peppers and Spinach

YIELDS 4 SERVINGS

8 cups purified water

2 cups chopped red onions

2 cups chopped red bell peppers

2 cups chopped yellow bell peppers

2 cups sliced button mushrooms

2 tablespoons ground cumin

2 tablespoons garlic powder

2 cups spinach

1. In a large pot, combine water, onion, peppers, mushrooms, and seasonings.

2. Over high heat, bring soup to a boil, reduce heat to a simmer, and cover.

3. Allow soup to simmer for 20 minutes or until all vegetables are tender.

4. Add spinach and stir until leaves are wilted and thoroughly combined, about 1–2 minutes.

5. Remove from heat and allow to cool.

6. Consume immediately or transfer soup to a large glass container with a tight-fitting lid. Soup can be stored in the refrigerator for up to 5 days or in the freezer for up to 1 month.

Per serving:
Calories: 136
Fat: 1.1 grams
Protein: 8.1 grams

Sodium: 126 milligrams
Carbohydrates: 26.8 grams
Sugar: 7.9 grams
Fiber: 7.2 grams

Peppered Quinoa

YIELDS 4 SERVINGS

8 cups purified water

2 cups chopped red bell peppers

2 cups chopped yellow bell peppers

2 cups chopped green bell peppers

2 cups minced red onions

4 tablespoons ground cumin

2 tablespoons garlic powder

2 cups cooked quinoa

1. In a large pot, combine all ingredients except quinoa.

2. Over high heat, bring soup to a boil, reduce heat to a simmer, and cover.

3. Allow soup to simmer for 30 minutes or until vegetables are tender.

4. Remove from heat and allow to cool for 5 minutes. Then stir in quinoa until thoroughly combined.

5. Consume immediately or transfer soup to a large glass container with a tight-fitting lid. Soup can be stored in the refrigerator for up to 5 days or in the freezer for up to 1 month.

Per serving:
Calories: 282
Fat: 1.4 grams
Protein: 10.4 grams

Sodium: 50 milligrams
Carbohydrates: 54.5 grams
Sugar: 10.3 grams
Fiber: 9.8 grams

Creamy Sweet Potato and Cauliflower

YIELDS 4 SERVINGS

8 cups unsweetened vanilla almond milk

4 large sweet potatoes, scrubbed and cubed into ¼" pieces

1 head cauliflower, chopped

2 tablespoons ground cinnamon

1 teaspoon ground cloves

1. In a large pot, combine all ingredients.

2. Over high heat, bring soup to a boil, reduce heat to a simmer, and cover.

3. Allow soup to simmer for 40 minutes or until all vegetables are fork-tender.

4. Remove from heat and allow to cool for 5 minutes.

5. Using an immersion blender, submerge blades in soup and blend on high until all ingredients are broken down and soup is well blended and desired consistency is achieved, about 5 minutes.

6. Consume immediately or transfer soup to a large glass container with a tight-fitting lid. Soup can be stored in the refrigerator for up to 5 days or in the freezer for up to 1 month.

Per serving:
Calories: 209
Fat: 5.2 grams
Protein: 6.3 grams
Sodium: 425 milligrams
Carbohydrates: 34.9 grams
Sugar: 7.6 grams
Fiber: 8.3 grams

Green Asparagus-Onion Blend

YIELDS 4 SERVINGS

8 cups purified water

4 cups asparagus spears

3 cups chopped Vidalia onions

3 cups spinach

2 tablespoons garlic powder

1. In a large pot, combine water, asparagus, and onion.

2. Over high heat, bring soup to a boil, reduce heat to a simmer, and cover.

3. Allow soup to simmer for 15 minutes or until asparagus and onion are tender.

4. Add spinach, stirring until all leaves are wilted and well blended, about 1–2 minutes.

5. Remove from heat and allow to cool.

6. Consume immediately or transfer soup to a large glass container with a tight-fitting lid. Soup can be stored in the refrigerator for up to 5 days or in the freezer for up to 1 month.

Per serving:
Calories: 120
Fat: 0.6 grams
Protein: 9.6 grams

Sodium: 169 milligrams
Carbohydrates: 24.1 grams
Sugar: 9.4 grams
Fiber: 8.1 grams

Fajita Quinoa

YIELDS 4 SERVINGS

8 cups purified water

2 cups chopped red bell peppers

2 cups chopped yellow bell peppers

2 cups chopped red onions

1 (15-ounce) can no-sodium black beans, rinsed

2 cups fresh corn kernels (may also use frozen and thawed)

4 tablespoons cumin powder

4 tablespoons garlic powder

2 cups cooked quinoa

1. In a large pot, combine water, peppers, onion, black beans, corn, cumin, and garlic powder.

2. Over high heat, bring soup to a boil, reduce heat to a simmer, and cover.

3. Allow soup to simmer for 30 minutes or until all ingredients are tender.

4. Remove from heat and stir in quinoa.

5. Consume immediately or transfer soup to a large glass container with a tight-fitting lid. Soup can be stored in the refrigerator for up to 5 days or in the freezer for up to 1 month.

Per serving:
Calories: 397
Fat: 2.7 grams
Protein: 16.9 grams

Sodium: 56 milligrams
Carbohydrates: 77.5 grams
Sugar: 10.3 grams
Fiber: 15.4 grams

Creamy Cajun Pepper-Mushroom

YIELDS 4 SERVINGS

8 cups unsweetened almond milk

2 cups chopped yellow bell peppers

2 cups chopped red bell peppers

2 cups chopped poblano peppers

4 cups sliced portobello mushrooms

4 tablespoons no-sodium blackening seasoning

2 tablespoons garlic powder

1. In a large pot, combine all ingredients.

2. Over high heat, bring soup to a boil, reduce heat to a simmer, and cover.

3. Allow soup to simmer for 20 minutes or until all vegetables are tender.

4. Remove from heat and allow to cool.

5. Consume immediately or transfer soup to a large glass container with a tight-fitting lid. Soup can be stored in the refrigerator for up to 5 days or in the freezer for up to 1 month.

Per serving:
Calories: 149
Fat: 5.4 grams
Protein: 6.6 grams

Sodium: 336 milligrams
Carbohydrates: 18.8 grams
Sugar: 6.8 grams
Fiber: 4.8 grams

Lime-Spiked Onion Soup with Tofu

YIELDS 4 SERVINGS

8 cups purified water

4 cups chopped red onions

4 cups chopped Vidalia onions

1 (16-ounce) package firm tofu, cubed into ¼" cubes

2 tablespoons garlic powder

1 cup freshly squeezed lime juice

1. In a large pot, combine water, red onion, Vidalia onion, tofu, and garlic powder.

2. Over high heat, bring soup to a boil, reduce heat to a simmer, and cover.

3. Allow soup to simmer for 15 minutes or until onions are tender.

4. Remove from heat, stir in lime juice, and mix well; then allow to cool.

5. Consume immediately or transfer soup to a large glass container with a tight-fitting lid. Soup can be stored in the refrigerator for up to 5 days or in the freezer for up to 1 month.

FILLING FIBER WITH FEW CALORIES

One of the best benefits of fiber-rich vegetables, especially the onions used in this recipe, is the stomach-filling effects that follow their consumption. By packing this vegetable into your favorite soups, you can enjoy delicious and nutritious servings of soup with few calories and tons of filling fiber that will keep you feeling full and satisfied!

Per serving:
Calories: 228
Fat: 4.5 grams
Protein: 12.9 grams

Sodium: 45 milligrams
Carbohydrates: 37.7 grams
Sugar: 16.2 grams
Fiber: 5.6 grams

Tomato-Basil Tofu

YIELDS 4 SERVINGS

8 cups purified water

8 cups stewed tomatoes

2 cups chopped basil leaves

4 tablespoons garlic powder

1 (16-ounce) package firm tofu, cubed into ¼" cubes

1. In a large pot, combine water, tomatoes, basil, and garlic powder.

2. Over high heat, bring soup to a boil, reduce heat to a simmer, and cover.

3. Allow soup to simmer for 30 minutes.

4. Remove from heat and allow to cool for 5 minutes.

5. Using an immersion blender, submerge blades and blend on high until all ingredients are broken down and thoroughly blended.

6. Add tofu, stirring to blend well.

7. Consume immediately or transfer soup to a large glass container with a tight-fitting lid. Soup can be stored in the refrigerator for up to 5 days or in the freezer for up to 1 month.

Per serving:

Calories: 277

Fat: 9.9 grams

Protein: 14.8 grams

Sodium: 948 milligrams

Carbohydrates: 35.6 grams

Sugar: 22.5 grams

Fiber: 5.3 grams

Vegetable Noodle

YIELDS 4 SERVINGS

8 cups purified water

3 cups chopped red onions

3 large carrots, peeled and chopped

4 celery ribs, chopped

2 tablespoons garlic powder

2 cups chopped spinach

1 (16-ounce) package rice noodles

1. In a large pot, combine water, onion, carrots, celery, and garlic powder.

2. Over high heat, bring soup to a boil, reduce heat to a simmer, and cover.

3. Allow soup to simmer for 20 minutes or until vegetables are tender.

4. Add spinach and noodles, stirring until spinach is wilted and noodles are tender, about 2 minutes.

5. Remove from heat and allow to cool.

6. Consume immediately or transfer soup to a large glass container with a tight-fitting lid. Soup can be stored in the refrigerator for up to 5 days or in the freezer for up to 1 month.

Per serving:
Calories: 533
Fat: 1.7 grams
Protein: 12.8 grams

Sodium: 303 milligrams
Carbohydrates: 118.0 grams
Sugar: 10.7 grams
Fiber: 8.6 grams

Broccoli-Cauliflower Cream

YIELDS 4 SERVINGS

8 cups almond milk

4 cups chopped broccoli florets

4 cups chopped cauliflower

1 cup chopped Vidalia onions

2 tablespoons garlic powder

1 tablespoon crushed black pepper

1. In a large pot, combine all ingredients.

2. Over high heat, bring soup to a boil, reduce heat to a simmer, and cover.

3. Allow soup to simmer for 30 minutes or until broccoli and cauliflower are tender.

4. Remove from heat and allow to cool for 5 minutes.

5. Using an immersion blender, submerge blades and blend soup on high until all ingredients are broken down and thoroughly combined, about 5 minutes.

6. Consume immediately or transfer soup to a large glass container with a tight-fitting lid. Soup can be stored in the refrigerator for up to 5 days or in the freezer for up to 1 month.

Per serving:
Calories: 199
Fat: 5.4 grams
Protein: 7.5 grams

Sodium: 377 milligrams
Carbohydrates: 32.7 grams
Sugar: 18.2 grams
Fiber: 3.4 grams

Asian Vegetable Soup

YIELDS 4 SERVINGS

8 cups plus 2 tablespoons purified water
2 cups chopped lemongrass
2 cups chopped red onions
2 large carrots, peeled, halved, and sliced
2 cups pea pods
2 garlic cloves, minced
2 tablespoons white miso paste

1. In a large pot, combine 8 cups water, lemongrass, onion, carrots, pea pods, and garlic.

2. Over high heat, bring soup to a boil, reduce heat to a simmer, and cover.

3. In a small bowl, whisk miso paste and remaining 2 tablespoons water until a smooth consistency is achieved. Add mixture to soup.

4. Allow soup to simmer for 20 minutes or until ingredients are tender.

5. Remove from heat and allow to cool.

6. Consume immediately or transfer soup to a large glass container with a tight-fitting lid. Soup can be stored in the refrigerator for up to 5 days or in the freezer for up to 1 month.

Per serving:
Calories: 195
Fat: 1.2 grams
Protein: 5.4 grams

Sodium: 427 milligrams
Carbohydrates: 45.4 grams
Sugar: 7.0 grams
Fiber: 3.8 grams

Creamy Pumpkin and Spice

YIELDS 4 SERVINGS

8 cups vanilla almond milk

4 cups ¼"-cubed pumpkin

1 (16-ounce) package silken tofu, cut into ¼" cubes

2 tablespoons ground cinnamon

1 tablespoon ground cloves

1 tablespoon powdered ginger

1. In a large pot, combine almond milk and pumpkin.

2. Over high heat, bring soup to a boil, reduce heat to a simmer, and cover.

3. Allow soup to simmer for 40 minutes or until pumpkin is fork-tender.

4. Remove from heat and allow to cool for 5 minutes.

5. Add tofu, cinnamon, cloves, and ginger.

6. Using an immersion blender, submerge blades and blend on high until all ingredients are broken down and blended thoroughly, about 5 minutes.

7. Consume immediately or transfer soup to a large glass container with a tight-fitting lid. Soup can be stored in the refrigerator for up to 5 days or in the freezer for up to 1 month.

Per serving:
Calories: 315
Fat: 7.9 grams
Protein: 9.6 grams
Sodium: 326 milligrams
Carbohydrates: 53.3 grams
Sugar: 35.3 grams
Fiber: 4.0 grams

CHAPTER 7

Immunity-Boosting Soups

Illness and disease can wreak havoc on the lives of anyone at any age. While prescriptions and over-the-counter medications were once the go-to solutions for health issues like the common cold, flus, allergies, and more, the world of alternative medicine restores health to the immune system via nutrient-rich whole foods like fruits, vegetables, and additions and has proven effective in preventing and treating illness. In this chapter, you'll find scrumptious sweet and savory combinations of nutrient-dense foods like spinach and kale, beets and citrus, and garlic and ginger that provide your body with essential vitamins like A, Bs, C, and E, and immunity-boosting minerals like iron, calcium, and potassium. These vitamins and minerals help ensure your body's needs are satisfied, which leaves your immune system free to focus on fighting illness and disease. Just as importantly, these soups are packed with ingredients full of potent phytochemicals that act as antioxidants, helping to protect the cells against cancerous changes, rid the body of harmful toxins, and prevent the infiltration of bacteria and viruses throughout the body. By eating for immunity with the cleansing soups found in this chapter—like the Lemon-Beet with Ginger, Tomato-Basil with Oregano Oil, Curry-Coconut-Lime Tofu, and Green Tea Cream—you can protect your body's cells and systems from the illnesses and disease that can negatively impact your health and quality of life.

Turmeric Tofu with Onions, Greens, and Lemongrass

YIELDS 4 SERVINGS

8 cups purified water

1 (16-ounce) package firm tofu, cut into ¼" cubes

2 cups chopped red onions

2 cups chopped lemongrass

2 cups chopped kale, ribs removed

4 tablespoons ground turmeric

3 tablespoons garlic powder

2 cups spinach

1. In a large pot, combine water, tofu, red onion, lemongrass, kale, turmeric, and garlic powder.

2. Over high heat, bring soup to a boil, reduce heat to a simmer, and cover.

3. Allow soup to simmer for 25 minutes or until all vegetables are tender.

4. Add spinach and stir until leaves are wilted, about 2 minutes.

5. Remove from heat and allow to cool.

6. Consume immediately or transfer soup to a large glass container with a tight-fitting lid. Soup can be stored in the refrigerator for up to 5 days or in the freezer for up to 1 month.

THE HEALING POWER OF TURMERIC

With a warm flavor that spices any savory dish to perfection, turmeric improves the flavor of dishes and your health as well. Packed with vitamins and minerals, the phytochemicals contained within turmeric act as potent antioxidants that help protect the cells and systems of the body against harmful free radicals, boosting the function of your immune system and protecting against illness and disease.

Per serving:
Calories: 240
Fat: 5.7 grams
Protein: 15.3 grams

Sodium: 66 milligrams
Carbohydrates: 31.9 grams
Sugar: 4.3 grams
Fiber: 5.8 grams

Lemon-Beet with Ginger

YIELDS 4 SERVINGS

8 cups purified water

3 red beets, chopped

3 golden beets, chopped

4" piece of ginger, peeled and chopped

½ cup freshly squeezed lemon juice

1. In a large pot, combine water, both kinds of beets, and ginger.

2. Over high heat, bring soup to a boil, reduce heat to a simmer, and cover.

3. Allow soup to simmer for 45 minutes or until beets are fork-tender.

4. Remove from heat, stir in lemon juice, and allow to cool.

5. Consume immediately or transfer soup to a large glass container with a tight-fitting lid. Soup can be stored in the refrigerator for up to 5 days or in the freezer for up to 1 month.

Per serving:

Calories: 80

Fat: 0.3 grams

Protein: 2.7 grams

Sodium: 137 milligrams

Carbohydrates: 18.5 grams

Sugar: 11.1 grams

Fiber: 4.5 grams

Tomato-Basil with Oregano Oil

YIELDS 4 SERVINGS

8 cups purified water

6 cups stewed tomatoes

4 cups chopped basil leaves

20 drops oregano oil

1. In a large pot, combine water, tomatoes, and basil.

2. Over high heat, bring soup to a boil, reduce heat to a simmer, and cover.

3. Allow soup to simmer for 20 minutes.

4. Remove from heat, add oregano oil, and allow to cool for 5 minutes.

5. Using an immersion blender, submerge blades and blend on high until all ingredients are broken down and thoroughly combined, about 5 minutes.

6. Consume immediately or transfer soup to a large glass container with a tight-fitting lid. Soup can be stored in the refrigerator for up to 5 days or in the freezer for up to 1 month.

Per serving:
Calories: 126
Fat: 4.26 grams
Protein: 3.8 grams

Sodium: 709 milligrams
Carbohydrates: 20.1 grams
Sugar: 16.6 grams
Fiber: 2.9 grams

Spinach, Spirulina, and Peppers

YIELDS 4 SERVINGS

8 cups purified water

2 cups chopped red bell peppers

2 cups chopped green bell peppers

2 tablespoons garlic powder

4 cups spinach

1 tablespoon spirulina

1. In a large pot, combine water, peppers, and garlic powder.

2. Over high heat, bring soup to a boil, reduce heat to a simmer, and cover.

3. Allow soup to simmer for 15 minutes or until vegetables are fork-tender.

4. Stir in spinach until leaves are wilted and well combined, about 1–2 minutes.

5. Remove from heat and allow to cool.

6. Stir in spirulina until evenly distributed throughout soup.

7. Consume immediately or transfer soup to a large glass container with a tight-fitting lid. Soup can be stored in the refrigerator for up to 5 days or in the freezer for up to 1 month.

SPIRULINA: AN ALGAE WITH COUNTLESS BENEFITS

Spirulina is one of the most nutrient-dense food sources. It provides tons of B vitamins, vitamin C, vitamin A; minerals like iron, calcium, and magnesium; and tons of protein, antioxidants, and immunity-boosting phytochemicals in every bioavailable teaspoon. Combined, these nutrients not only protect the cells from damage, improve energy and metabolic functioning, and support nervous system functioning, but they also help the body maintain a balance of mineral levels (like iron, potassium, and magnesium) that ensures all systems function optimally. As soon as this simple algae is consumed, it hits the bloodstream and is quickly dispersed throughout the body, providing immediate health benefits that keep your immune system on track.

Per serving:
Calories: 111
Fat: 0.8 grams
Protein: 9.8 grams

Sodium: 226 milligrams
Carbohydrates: 20.2 grams
Sugar: 6.1 grams
Fiber: 8.4 grams

Three-Onion Miso

YIELDS 4 SERVINGS

8 cups plus 2 tablespoons purified water

2 cups chopped red onions

2 cups chopped Vidalia onions

2 cups chopped green onions

2 garlic cloves, chopped

2 tablespoons white miso paste

2 cups spinach

1. In a large pot, combine 8 cups water, all the onions, and garlic.

2. Over high heat, bring soup to a boil, reduce heat to a simmer, and cover.

3. Allow soup to simmer for 20 minutes or until onions are tender.

4. In a small bowl, whisk miso paste and 2 tablespoons water until creamy and add to soup.

5. Add spinach and stir until leaves are wilted and well-combined, about 1–2 minutes.

6. Remove from heat and allow to cool.

7. Consume immediately or transfer soup to a large glass container with a tight-fitting lid. Soup can be stored in the refrigerator for up to 5 days or in the freezer for up to 1 month.

Per serving:
Calories: 123
Fat: 1.0 grams
Protein: 7.0 grams

Sodium: 500 milligrams
Carbohydrates: 24.8 grams
Sugar: 10.0 grams
Fiber: 6.5 grams

Curried Chicken, Noodle, and Vegetable

YIELDS 4 SERVINGS

8 cups purified water

2 cups sliced red onion

2 carrots, peeled and chopped

4 celery ribs, chopped

4 tablespoons curry powder

2 tablespoons garlic powder

2 cups chopped cooked chicken

1 (16-ounce) package rice noodles

1. In a large pot, combine water, onion, carrot, and celery; then season with curry and garlic powder.

2. Over high heat, bring soup to a boil, reduce heat to a simmer, and cover.

3. Allow soup to simmer for 20 minutes or until vegetables are tender.

4. Add chicken and rice noodles and stir until chicken is distributed throughout soup and rice noodles are tender, about 2 minutes.

5. Remove from heat and allow to cool.

6. Consume immediately or transfer soup to a large glass container with a tight-fitting lid. Soup can be stored in the refrigerator for up to 5 days or in the freezer for up to 1 month.

Per serving:
Calories: 599
Fat: 4.4 grams
Protein: 28.4 grams

Sodium: 233 milligrams
Carbohydrates: 109.4 grams
Sugar: 6.6 grams
Fiber: 6.5 grams

Cinnamon Apples and Pears with Ginger

YIELDS 4 SERVINGS

8 cups vanilla almond milk

4 Fuji apples, peeled, cored, and chopped

2 Bartlett pears, peeled, cored, and chopped

3" piece of ginger, peeled and sliced

4 tablespoons ground cinnamon

1. In a large pot, combine all ingredients.

2. Over high heat, bring soup to a boil, reduce heat to a simmer, and cover.

3. Allow soup to simmer for 20 minutes, or until apples and pears are fork-tender.

4. Remove from heat and allow to cool for 5 minutes.

5. Using an immersion blender, submerge blades and blend on high until all ingredients are broken down and thoroughly combined, about 5 minutes.

6. Consume immediately or transfer soup to a large glass container with a tight-fitting lid. Soup can be stored in the refrigerator for up to 5 days or in the freezer for up to 1 month.

Per serving:

Calories: 283

Fat: 5.2 grams

Protein: 2.9 grams

Sodium: 321 milligrams

Carbohydrates: 60.4 grams

Sugar: 48.6 grams

Fiber: 6.4 grams

Lemon-Lime Pineapple Quinoa

YIELDS 4 SERVINGS

4 cups vanilla almond milk

2 cups kefir

2 cups pineapple juice

½ cup freshly squeezed lemon juice

½ cup freshly squeezed lime juice

3 cups chopped pineapple

2 cups cooked quinoa

1. In a large pot, combine almond milk, kefir, pineapple juice, lemon juice, lime juice, and pineapple.

2. Using an immersion blender, submerge blades and blend on high until the pineapple is broken down and the ingredients are thoroughly combined, about 5 minutes.

3. Stir in quinoa until well blended, about 1 minute.

4. Consume immediately or transfer soup to a large glass container with a tight-fitting lid. Soup can be stored in the refrigerator for up to 5 days or in the freezer for up to 1month.

Per serving:
Calories: 474
Fat: 6.72 grams
Protein: 11.7 grams

Sodium: 235 milligrams
Carbohydrates: 91.2 grams
Sugar: 52.7 grams
Fiber: 7.6 grams

Herbed Lemon Sweet Cream

YIELDS 4 SERVINGS

4 cups almond milk

2 cups Greek yogurt

2 cups vanilla kefir

1 cup freshly squeezed lemon juice

2 cups chopped fresh basil

1. In a countertop blender, combine all ingredients.

2. Blend on high until all ingredients are broken down and thoroughly combined, about 2–3 minutes.

3. Consume immediately or transfer soup to a large glass container with a tight-fitting lid. Soup can be stored in the refrigerator for up to 5 days or in the freezer for up to 1 month.

Per serving:
Calories: 251
Fat: 9.6 grams
Protein: 14.6 grams

Sodium: 238 milligrams
Carbohydrates: 29.5 grams
Sugar: 24.1 grams
Fiber: 1.4 grams

Spicy Peppers with Oregano Oil

8 cups purified water

2 cups chopped red bell peppers

2 cups chopped yellow bell peppers

2 cups chopped green bell peppers

2 garlic cloves, minced

¼ teaspoon cayenne pepper

20 drops oregano oil

1. In a large pot, combine water, peppers, and garlic.

2. Over high heat, bring soup to a boil, reduce heat to a simmer, and cover.

3. Allow soup to simmer for 15 minutes or until peppers are tender.

4. Remove from heat and allow to cool for 15 minutes.

5. Add cayenne pepper and oregano oil and stir to combine well.

6. Consume immediately or transfer soup to a large glass container with a tight-fitting lid. Soup can be stored in the refrigerator for up to 5 days or in the freezer for up to 1 month.

THE SURPRISING BENEFITS OF OREGANO OIL

Oregano oil is the condensed extraction of the oregano plant, and it has been used for centuries by countless cultures in the pursuit of better health. With every drop providing the body with natural antioxidants plus antibacterial, antiviral, and antimicrobial benefits that help improve the strength of the immune system, safeguard cells from harmful changes, and ensure the proper storage and use of essential nutrients, this simple addition can be added to your favorite soups, improving the flavor and health benefits of every last sip!

Per serving:
Calories: 62
Fat: 0.3 grams
Protein: 2.3 grams

Sodium: 25 milligrams
Carbohydrates: 13.5 grams
Sugar: 5.0 grams
Fiber: 3.6 grams

Honey-Ginger-Turmeric Tofu

YIELDS 4 SERVINGS

8 cups purified water

1 cup organic all-natural honey

3" piece of ginger, peeled and chopped

4 tablespoons ground turmeric

1 (16-ounce) package firm tofu, cubed into ¼" pieces

1. In a large pot, combine all ingredients.

2. Over high heat, bring soup to a boil, reduce heat to a simmer, and cover.

3. Allow soup to simmer for 20 minutes or until ginger is tender.

4. Remove from heat and allow to cool.

5. Consume immediately or transfer soup to a large glass container with a tight-fitting lid. Soup can be stored in the refrigerator for up to 5 days or in the freezer for up to 1 month.

GINGER'S IMMUNITY-BOOSTING PHYTOCHEMICALS

With unique oils, enzymes, and phytochemicals that act as powerful antioxidants, ginger not only adds delightful spice to your favorite soups, but it also supports the immune system's functioning. Acting as antibacterial, antiviral, and antimicrobial agents, the phytochemicals of ginger help the immune system by cleansing the blood and the body's cells and systems of harmful microbes that can cause colds, flus, and more serious infections and harmful changes within the systems!

Per serving:
Calories: 380
Fat: 5.0 grams
Protein: 9.9 grams

Sodium: 30 milligrams
Carbohydrates: 79.8 grams
Sugar: 70.3 grams
Fiber: 3.1 grams

Curry-Coconut-Lime Tofu

YIELDS 4 SERVINGS

7 cups unsweetened coconut milk

1 cup freshly squeezed lime juice

4 tablespoons curry powder

1 (16-ounce) package firm tofu, cubed into ¼" pieces

1. In a large pot, combine all ingredients.
2. Over high heat, bring soup to a boil, reduce heat to a simmer, and cover.
3. Allow soup to simmer for 10 minutes.
4. Remove from heat and allow to cool.
5. Consume immediately or transfer soup to a large glass container with a tight-fitting lid. Soup can be stored in the refrigerator for up to 5 days or in the freezer for up to 1 month.

Per serving:
Calories: 196
Fat: 12.0 grams
Protein: 9.8 grams
Sodium: 69 milligrams
Carbohydrates: 10.8 grams
Sugar: 1.4 grams
Fiber: 3.1 grams

Tom-Kha-Gai Soup

YIELDS 4 SERVINGS

4 cups Spicy Thai Chicken Broth (see Chapter 10)

4 cups coconut milk

3 2" pieces of ginger, peeled and chopped

2 cups shredded chicken

2 cups sliced mushrooms

1 cup chopped lemongrass

¼ cup lime juice

3 tablespoons Thai chili paste

1 cup chopped fresh basil

1 cup chopped fresh cilantro

1. In a large pot, combine all ingredients except basil and cilantro and stir.
2. Over high heat, bring soup to a boil, reduce heat to a simmer, and cover.
3. Allow soup to simmer for 30 minutes.
4. Remove from heat and allow to cool for 5 minutes; stir in basil and cilantro until thoroughly combined.
5. Consume immediately or transfer soup to a large glass container with a tight-fitting lid. Soup can be stored in the refrigerator for up to 5 days or in the freezer for up to 1 month.

Per serving:
Calories: 274
Fat: 10.6 grams
Protein: 25.5 grams
Sodium: 597 milligrams
Carbohydrates: 22.0 grams
Sugar: 11.7 grams
Fiber: 1.3 grams

Basil-Thai Miso

YIELDS 4 SERVINGS

8 cups plus 2 tablespoons purified water

2 cups chopped scallions

2 cups chopped lemongrass

4 cups chopped fresh basil

2 tablespoons white miso paste

1. In a large pot, combine 8 cups water, scallions, lemongrass, and basil.

2. Over high heat, bring soup to a boil, reduce heat to a simmer, and cover.

3. Allow soup to simmer for 15 minutes or until lemongrass is tender.

4. In a small bowl, whisk miso paste and 2 tablespoons water until thoroughly combined and creamy. Add to soup and stir to blend well.

5. Remove from heat and allow to cool.

6. Consume immediately or transfer soup to a large glass container with a tight-fitting lid. Soup can be stored in the refrigerator for up to 5 days or in the freezer for up to 1 month.

Per serving:
Calories: 74
Fat: 0.9 grams
Protein: 3.4 grams

Sodium: 402 milligrams
Carbohydrates: 15.4 grams
Sugar: 1.8 grams
Fiber: 2.2 grams

Green Onion Quinoa

YIELDS 4 SERVINGS

8 cups purified water

2 cups chopped Vidalia onions

3 cups chopped scallions

4 cups chopped spinach

2 cups cooked quinoa

1. In a large pot, combine water, onions, and scallions.

2. Over high heat, bring soup to a boil, reduce heat to a simmer, and cover.

3. Allow soup to simmer for 20 minutes or until Vidalia onions are softened.

4. Add spinach and quinoa and stir until spinach leaves are wilted and quinoa is well combined, about 1–2 minutes.

5. Remove from heat and allow to cool.

6. Consume immediately or transfer soup to a large glass container with a tight-fitting lid. Soup can be stored in the refrigerator for up to 5 days or in the freezer for up to 1 month.

Per serving:
Calories: 240
Fat: 0.7 grams
Protein: 13.7 grams

Sodium: 226 milligrams
Carbohydrates: 44.4 grams
Sugar: 6.7 grams
Fiber: 11.0 grams

Sweet Onions and Peppers with Greens

YIELDS 4 SERVINGS

8 cups purified water

2 cups sliced Vidalia onions

2 cups sliced red onions

2 cups sliced red bell peppers

1 cup chopped kale, ribs removed

2 cups spinach

1. In a large pot, combine water, onions, peppers, and kale.

2. Over high heat, bring soup to a boil, reduce heat to a simmer, and cover.

3. Allow soup to simmer for 20 minutes or until vegetables are tender.

4. Add spinach and stir until leaves are wilted, about 1–2 minutes.

5. Remove from heat and allow to cool.

6. Consume immediately or transfer soup to a large glass container with a tight-fitting lid. Soup can be stored in the refrigerator for up to 5 days or in the freezer for up to 1 month.

Per serving:
Calories: 90
Fat: 0.4 grams
Protein: 5.4 grams

Sodium: 125 milligrams
Carbohydrates: 18.3 grams
Sugar: 7.5 grams
Fiber: 5.3 grams

Roasted Reds Soup

YIELDS 4 SERVINGS

¼ cup extra-virgin olive oil

3 cups sliced red onions

3 cups chopped red bell peppers

2 cups chopped red kale

4 garlic cloves

8 cups purified water

1. Preheat oven to 400°F.

2. Prepare a baking sheet or roasting pan by drizzling olive oil to coat; scatter the onions, peppers, kale, and garlic cloves evenly on the pan.

3. Roast vegetables for 40 minutes, turning once after 20 minutes to roast evenly.

4. Transfer roasted vegetables to a large pot and cover with water.

5. Over high heat, bring soup to a boil, reduce heat to a simmer, and cover.

6. Allow soup to simmer for 20 minutes.

7. Remove from heat and allow to cool.

8. Consume immediately or transfer soup to a large glass container with a tight-fitting lid. Soup can be stored in the refrigerator for up to 5 days or in the freezer for up to 1 month.

Per serving:

Calories: 179

Fat: 10.2 grams

Protein: 3.4 grams

Sodium: 41 milligrams

Carbohydrates: 19.1 grams

Sugar: 8.4 grams

Fiber: 4.6 grams

Green Tea Cream

YIELDS 4 SERVINGS

5 cups prepared green tea

4" piece of ginger, peeled and sliced

2 tablespoons maple syrup

3 cups kefir

1. In a large pot, combine green tea and ginger.

2. Over high heat, bring soup to a boil, reduce heat to a simmer, and cover.

3. Allow soup to simmer for 30 minutes or until ginger is tender.

4. Remove from heat and allow to cool for 1 hour.

5. Add maple syrup and kefir.

6. Using an immersion blender, submerge blades and blend on high until all ingredients are broken down and thoroughly combined, about 5 minutes.

7. Consume immediately or transfer soup to a large glass container with a tight-fitting lid. Soup can be stored in the refrigerator for up to 5 days or in the freezer for up to 1 month.

Per serving:

Calories: 151

Fat: 6.1 grams

Protein: 6.2 grams

Sodium: 98 milligrams

Carbohydrates: 18.7 grams

Sugar: 13.5 grams

Fiber: 2.5 grams

Sweet Beets and Spice

YIELDS 4 SERVINGS

4 tablespoons coconut oil, divided

4 red beets, washed and sliced

4 gold beets, washed and sliced

2" piece of ginger, peeled and sliced

1 tablespoon ground cinnamon

1 tablespoon ground cardamom

1 teaspoon ground cloves

2 tablespoons maple syrup

4 cups purified water

4 cups organic apple juice (not from concentrate)

1. Preheat oven to 400°F.

2. Prepare a baking sheet or roasting pan by drizzling 2 tablespoons coconut oil to coat, then scatter the beets and ginger evenly about the pan. Drizzle the remaining 2 tablespoons coconut oil over the beets and ginger and season with the cinnamon, cardamom, cloves, and maple syrup.

3. Roast vegetables for 40 minutes, turning once after 20 minutes to roast evenly.

4. Transfer roasted vegetables to a large pot and cover with water and apple juice.

5. Over high heat, bring soup to a boil, reduce heat to a simmer, and cover.

6. Allow soup to simmer for 20 minutes.

7. Remove from heat and allow to cool for 5 minutes.

8. Using an immersion blender, submerge blades and blend on high until all ingredients are broken down and thoroughly combined, about 5 minutes.

9. Consume immediately or transfer soup to a large glass container with a tight-fitting lid. Soup can be stored in the refrigerator for up to 5 days or in the freezer for up to 1 month.

SPICES WITH BENEFITS

Adding teaspoons of cinnamon, cloves, and cardamom can improve the immunity-boosting benefits of your dishes as well as the flavor! Helping to fight free radicals, bacteria, viruses, and microbes, the naturally occurring phytochemicals of spices help keep your immune system strong.

Per serving:
Calories: 321
Fat: 10.2 grams
Protein: 3.8 grams

Sodium: 178 milligrams
Carbohydrates: 55.8 grams
Sugar: 41.8 grams
Fiber: 7.8 grams

Curried Roasted Root Vegetable Bisque

YIELDS 4 SERVINGS

½ cup extra-virgin olive oil, divided

2 large carrots, peeled and chopped

4 celery ribs, chopped

2 large sweet potatoes, scrubbed and chopped

1 large turnip, peeled and chopped

1 cup chopped red onions

4 tablespoons curry powder

8 cups unsweetened almond milk

1. Preheat oven to 400°F.

2. Prepare a baking sheet or roasting pan by drizzling ¼ cup olive oil to coat, then scatter the carrots, celery, sweet potatoes, turnip, and red onion evenly throughout the pan. Drizzle the vegetables with the remaining ¼ cup olive oil and season with the curry powder.

3. Roast vegetables for 40 minutes, turning once after 20 minutes to roast evenly.

4. Transfer roasted vegetables to a large pot and cover with the almond milk.

5. Over high heat, bring soup to a boil, reduce heat to a simmer, and cover.

6. Allow soup to simmer for 20 minutes.

7. Remove from heat and allow to cool for 5 minutes.

8. Using an immersion blender, submerge blades and blend on high until all ingredients are broken down and thoroughly combined, about 5 minutes.

9. Consume immediately or transfer soup to a large glass container with a tight-fitting lid. Soup can be stored in the refrigerator for up to 5 days or in the freezer for up to 1 month.

Per serving:
Calories: 359
Fat: 23.5 grams
Protein: 5.9 grams
Sodium: 521 milligrams
Carbohydrates: 30.8 grams
Sugar: 10.5 grams
Fiber: 8.7 grams

CHAPTER 8

Healthy Gut Soups

Few people realize how important gut health can be, not only to the frequency or intensity of stomach issues but to the systems and functioning of the entire body! Responsible for the absorption, processing, and distribution of the very nutrients your body requires to function, the gut is the first line of defense against illness, and is the precise place where carbohydrate, fat, and protein metabolism begins. For countless reasons, any diet focused on achieving better health should prioritize the nutrients needed to promote gut health.

Fortunately, with clean sources of quality nutrients like fruits and vegetables, healthy additions like probiotic-rich kefir and protein-packed yogurt, and spices like garlic and ginger, the recipes found in this chapter are delicious additions to any gut-focused diet routine. Packed with vibrant vegetables and tasty fruits that are full of B vitamins and vitamins A, C, E, and K, as well as minerals like iron, magnesium, potassium, and selenium, these antioxidant-rich ingredients combine with protein- and probiotic-rich additions that help maintain a healthy balance of beneficial bacteria, protect against illness and disruption to the gut's environment, and improve the functioning of the countless processes performed by the gut. Delicious and nutritious, recipes like Stir-Fry Soup, Sweet Potato Split-Pea, Roasted Red Pepper with Rosemary, and Spiced Green Asparagus Cream make achieving a healthier gut quick, easy, and simply delicious!

Creamy Gingered Cabbage with Kefir

YIELDS 4 SERVINGS

6 cups unsweetened vanilla almond milk

6 cups chopped red cabbage

4" piece of ginger, peeled and chopped

2 cups kefir

1. In a large pot, combine almond milk, cabbage, and ginger.

2. Over high heat, bring soup to a boil, reduce heat to a simmer, and cover.

3. Allow soup to simmer for 20 minutes or until cabbage and ginger are tender.

4. Remove from heat and allow to cool for 4 hours.

5. Add kefir to cooled soup.

6. Using an immersion blender, submerge blades and blend on high until all ingredients are broken down and thoroughly blended, about 5 minutes.

7. Consume immediately or transfer soup to a large glass container with a tight-fitting lid. Soup can be stored in the refrigerator for up to 5 days or in the freezer for up to 1 month.

KEFIR'S POWERFUL PROBIOTICS

Kefir is a probiotic-rich, yogurt-like drink that includes just the slightest amount of lactose, making it tolerable for most of those who struggle with lactose digestion. With a variety of potent probiotic bacteria such as *Lactobacillus acidophilus, Bifidobacterium bifidum, Streptococcus thermophilus, Lactobacillus delbrueckii* subsp. *bulgaricus, Lactobacillus helveticus, Lactobacillus kefiranofaciens,* and *Lactococcus lactis,* kefir soothes digestive issues, promotes the healthy levels of good bacteria in the gut, and helps restore regularity. Possibly the simplest way to improve your health while adding sweetness to any soup, kefir is the perfect addition to your daily soup cleanse routine.

Per serving:
Calories: 176
Fat: 8.0 grams
Protein: 7.6 grams

Sodium: 340 milligrams
Carbohydrates: 19.4 grams
Sugar: 11.3 grams
Fiber: 4.5 grams

Deep-Green Green-Tea Soup

YIELDS 4 SERVINGS

4 cups purified water

4 cups prepared green tea

2 cups chopped kale, ribs removed

2 cups chopped green cabbage

2 cups chopped red onions

4 cups spinach

¼ cup apple cider vinegar

1. In a large pot, combine water, tea, kale, cabbage, and red onion.

2. Over high heat, bring soup to a boil, reduce heat to a simmer, and cover.

3. Allow soup to simmer for 30 minutes or until vegetables are tender.

4. Add spinach and stir until leaves are wilted and well combined, about 1–2 minutes.

5. Remove from heat and allow to cool for 20 minutes. Add apple cider vinegar and stir to blend well.

6. Consume immediately or transfer soup to a large glass container with a tight-fitting lid. Soup can be stored in the refrigerator for up to 5 days or in the freezer for up to 1 month.

ALKALIZING GREENS

One of the best benefits of a diet rich in greens like spinach and kale is the improvement of gut health. The alkalizing properties of greens help restore a healthy pH balance to the digestive system, improving digestion and relieving a number of stomach issues. Whether you suffer from digestive issues regularly or infrequently, the addition of alkalizing greens to your daily soup-cleansing routine can improve your health and quality of life quickly, easily, and deliciously!

Per serving:
Calories: 117
Fat: 0.8 grams
Protein: 9.1 grams

Sodium: 55 milligrams
Carbohydrates: 22.4 grams
Sugar: 5.8 grams
Fiber: 8.2 grams

Radish, Red Onion, Greens, and Ginger

YIELDS 4 SERVINGS

8 cups purified water

2 cups thinly sliced red radishes

2 cups thinly sliced red onion

2 cups chopped kale, ribs removed

3" piece of ginger, peeled and minced

2 cups spinach

1. In a large pot, combine water, radishes, red onion, kale, and ginger.

2. Over high heat, bring soup to a boil, reduce heat to a simmer, and cover.

3. Allow soup to simmer for 30 minutes or until all vegetables are tender.

4. Add spinach, stirring until leaves are wilted and all ingredients are well combined, about 1–2 minutes.

5. Remove from heat and allow to cool.

6. Consume immediately or transfer soup to a large glass container with a tight-fitting lid. Soup can be stored in the refrigerator for up to 5 days or in the freezer for up to 1 month.

Per serving:
Calories: 82
Fat: 0.6 grams
Protein: 5.6 grams

Sodium: 65 milligrams
Carbohydrates: 16.4 grams
Sugar: 4.2 grams
Fiber: 5.3 grams

Creamed Kale, Spinach, and Onion

YIELDS 4 SERVINGS

8 cups unsweetened almond milk

2 cups chopped kale, ribs removed

3 cups chopped Vidalia onions

3 cups chopped spinach

1 tablespoon ground nutmeg

1. In a large pot, combine almond milk, kale, and onion.

2. Over high heat, bring soup to a boil, reduce heat to a simmer, and cover.

3. Allow soup to simmer for 20 minutes or until kale and onion are tender.

4. Add spinach and nutmeg and stir until spinach is wilted, about 1–2 minutes.

5. Remove from heat and allow to cool for 5 minutes.

6. Using an immersion blender, submerge blades and blend on high until all ingredients are broken down and thoroughly combined, about 5 minutes.

7. Consume immediately or transfer soup to a large glass container with a tight-fitting lid. Soup can be stored in the refrigerator for up to 5 days or in the freezer for up to 1 month.

FIBER FOR GUT HEALTH

When you consume fiber-rich foods like fruits, vegetables, nuts, and seeds, the fiber within the foods turns to a gel-like substance within the digestive system. Moving through the colon, the fiber cleans every nook and cranny in its path. As the fibrous gel is digested, it helps sweep undigested particles that can wreak havoc on your health out of your system, helping to keep your entire body in great shape.

Per serving:

Calories: 163

Fat: 6.1 grams

Protein: 9.1 grams

Sodium: 480 milligrams

Carbohydrates: 19.5 grams

Sugar: 7.3 grams

Fiber: 5.9 grams

Spiced Green Asparagus Cream

YIELDS 4 SERVINGS

8 cups unsweetened almond milk

4 cups asparagus spears

2 cups chopped kale, ribs removed

4 garlic cloves

2 cups spinach

1. In a large pot, combine almond milk, asparagus, kale, and garlic.

2. Over high heat, bring soup to a boil, reduce heat to a simmer, and cover.

3. Allow soup to simmer for 20 minutes or until asparagus, kale, and garlic cloves are tender.

4. Add spinach and stir until leaves are wilted, about 1–2 minutes.

5. Remove from heat and allow to cool for 5 minutes.

6. Using an immersion blender, submerge blades and blend on high until ingredients are broken down and thoroughly combined, about 5 minutes.

7. Consume immediately or transfer soup to a large glass container with a tight-fitting lid. Soup can be stored in the refrigerator for up to 5 days or in the freezer for up to 1 month.

Per serving:
Calories: 134
Fat: 5.8 grams
Protein: 9.5 grams
Sodium: 428 milligrams
Carbohydrates: 13.7 grams
Sugar: 3.0 grams
Fiber: 6.1 grams

Roasted Red Onion and Tomato with Basil and Garlic

YIELDS 4 SERVINGS

½ cup extra-virgin olive oil, divided

3 cups chopped red onions

6 Roma tomatoes, sliced

6 garlic cloves, chopped

8 cups purified water

2 cups chopped fresh basil

1. Preheat oven to 400°F.

2. Prepare a baking sheet or roasting pan by drizzling ¼ cup olive oil to coat. Evenly distribute the onions, tomatoes, and garlic cloves in the pan and drizzle with remaining ¼ cup olive oil.

3. Roast vegetables for 40 minutes, turning after 20 minutes.

4. Transfer vegetables and drippings to a large pot and cover with water.

5. Over high heat, bring soup to a boil, reduce heat to a simmer, and cover.

6. Allow soup to simmer for 20 minutes.

7. Remove from heat, add basil, and allow to cool for 5 minutes.

8. Using an immersion blender, submerge blades and blend on high until all ingredients are broken down and thoroughly combined, about 5 minutes.

9. Consume immediately or transfer soup to a large glass container with a tight-fitting lid. Soup can be stored in the refrigerator for up to 5 days or in the freezer for up to 1 month.

Per serving:
Calories: 292
Fat: 21.4 grams
Protein: 3.7 grams

Sodium: 32 milligrams
Carbohydrates: 24.4 grams
Sugar: 14.2 grams
Fiber: 3.9 grams

Cardamom Cashew Cream with Flax

YIELDS 4 SERVINGS

8 cups vanilla almond milk

4 cups raw cashews

4 tablespoons ground cardamom

½ cup ground flaxseed

1. In a large pot, combine almond milk, cashews, and cardamom.

2. Over high heat, bring soup to a boil, reduce heat to a simmer, and cover.

3. Allow soup to simmer for 20 minutes or until cashews are softened.

4. Remove from heat, add flaxseed, and allow to cool for 5 minutes.

5. Using an immersion blender, submerge blades and blend on high until all ingredients are broken down and thoroughly combined, about 5 minutes.

6. Consume immediately or transfer soup to a large glass container with a tight-fitting lid. Soup can be stored in the refrigerator for up to 5 days or in the freezer for up to 1 month.

Per serving:
Calories: 1101
Fat: 77.1 grams
Protein: 32.0 grams

Sodium: 343 milligrams
Carbohydrates: 85.4 grams
Sugar: 40.9 grams
Fiber: 10.6 grams

Red Peppered Cabbage with Apple Cider Vinegar

YIELDS 4 SERVINGS

8 cups purified water

4 cups chopped red cabbage

2 cups chopped red onions

2 cups chopped red bell peppers

¼ cup organic unfiltered apple cider vinegar

1. In a large pot, combine water, cabbage, red onion, and red peppers.

2. Over high heat, bring soup to a boil, reduce heat to a simmer, and cover.

3. Allow soup to simmer for 20 minutes or until vegetables are softened.

4. Remove from heat and allow to cool for 1 hour.

5. Add apple cider vinegar and stir to combine thoroughly.

6. Consume immediately or transfer soup to a large glass container with a tight-fitting lid. Soup can be stored in the refrigerator for up to 5 days or in the freezer for up to 1 month.

Per serving:
Calories: 85
Fat: 0.2 grams
Protein: 2.9 grams

Sodium: 49 milligrams
Carbohydrates: 18.7 grams
Sugar: 10.0 grams
Fiber: 4.8 grams

Fiber-Filled Greens with Ginger and Nutmeg

YIELDS 4 SERVINGS

8 cups purified water

2 cups asparagus spears

2 cups chopped green cabbage

2 cups chopped kale, ribs removed

4" piece of ginger, peeled and chopped

1 tablespoon ground nutmeg

4 cups spinach

¼ cup ground flaxseed

1. In a large pot, combine water, asparagus, cabbage, kale, ginger, and nutmeg.

2. Over high heat, bring soup to a boil, reduce heat to a simmer, and cover.

3. Allow soup to simmer for 20 minutes.

4. Add spinach and flaxseed and stir until spinach leaves are wilted, about 1–2 minutes.

5. Remove from heat and allow to cool for 5 minutes.

6. Using an immersion blender, submerge blades and blend on high until all ingredients are broken down and thoroughly combined, about 5 minutes.

7. Consume immediately or transfer soup to a large glass container with a tight-fitting lid. Soup can be stored in the refrigerator for up to 5 days or in the freezer for up to 1 month.

Per serving:
Calories: 149
Fat: 4.4 grams
Protein: 11.0 grams

Sodium: 51 milligrams
Carbohydrates: 21.8 grams
Sugar: 4.4 grams
Fiber: 10.8 grams

Spinach and Spirulina Tomato Miso

YIELDS 4 SERVINGS

8 cups plus 2 tablespoons purified water

6 cups spinach

6 cups stewed tomatoes

3 garlic cloves

1 tablespoon spirulina

2 tablespoons red miso paste

1. In a blender, combine 8 cups water, spinach, tomatoes, garlic, and spirulina.

2. In a separate dish, whisk miso paste and 2 tablespoons water until creamy and thoroughly combined.

3. Add miso mixture to soup.

4. Blend on high until all ingredients are broken down and thoroughly combined, about 5 minutes.

5. Consume immediately or transfer soup to a large glass container with a tight-fitting lid. Soup can be stored in the refrigerator for up to 5 days or in the freezer for up to 1 month.

Per serving:
Calories: 227
Fat: 5.6 grams
Protein: 15.2 grams
Sodium: 1117 milligrams

Carbohydrates: 35.8 grams
Sugar: 18.6 grams
Fiber: 10.8 grams

Asparagus and Cabbage in Bone Broth

YIELDS 4 SERVINGS

8 cups Traditional Vegetable-Based Chicken Broth (see Chapter 10)

4 cups asparagus spears

4 cups chopped green cabbage

2 cups chopped red cabbage

4 garlic cloves, minced

1. In a large pot, combine all ingredients.

2. Over high heat, bring soup to a boil, reduce heat to a simmer, and cover.

3. Allow soup to simmer for 30 minutes or until vegetables are tender.

4. Remove from heat and allow to cool.

5. Consume immediately or transfer soup to a large glass container with a tight-fitting lid. Soup can be stored in the refrigerator for up to 5 days or in the freezer for up to 1 month.

Per serving:
Calories: 113
Fat: 1.8 grams
Protein: 7.9 grams

Sodium: 87 milligrams
Carbohydrates: 19.4 grams
Sugar: 9.5 grams
Fiber: 6.6 grams

Creamy Carrot, Broccoli, and Spinach

YIELDS 4 SERVINGS

8 cups unsweetened almond milk

4 large carrots, peeled and chopped

2 cups broccoli spears

3 cups spinach

½ cup ground flaxseed

1. In a large pot, combine almond milk, carrots, and broccoli.

2. Over high heat, bring soup to a boil, reduce heat to a simmer, and cover.

3. Allow soup to simmer for 25 minutes or until carrots are tender.

4. Add spinach and flaxseed and stir until spinach leaves are wilted, about 1–2 minutes.

5. Remove from heat and allow to cool for 5 minutes.

6. Using an immersion blender, submerge blades and blend on high until all ingredients are broken down and thoroughly combined, about 5 minutes.

7. Consume immediately or transfer soup to a large glass container with a tight-fitting lid. Soup can be stored in the refrigerator for up to 5 days or in the freezer for up to 1 month.

Per serving:

Calories: 215

Fat: 11.6 grams

Protein: 11.0 grams

Sodium: 414 milligrams

Carbohydrates: 19.6 grams

Sugar: 4.8 grams

Fiber: 11.2 grams

Tofu Vegetable Noodle

YIELDS 4 SERVINGS

8 cups purified water

2 carrots, peeled and diced

3 celery ribs, chopped

1 cup chopped red onions

1 cup chopped Vidalia onions

1 cup chopped kale leaves, ribs removed

1 (16-ounce) package firm tofu, cut into ¼" cubes

4 garlic cloves, minced

2 cups spinach

1 (16-ounce) package rice noodles

1. In a large pot, combine water, carrots, celery, onions, kale, tofu, and garlic.

2. Over high heat, bring soup to a boil, reduce heat to a simmer, and cover.

3. Allow soup to simmer for 30 minutes or until vegetables are softened.

4. Add spinach and rice noodles and stir until spinach leaves are wilted and noodles are tender, about 1–2 minutes.

5. Remove from heat and allow to cool.

6. Consume immediately or transfer soup to a large glass container with a tight-fitting lid. Soup can be stored in the refrigerator for up to 5 days or in the freezer for up to 1 month.

Per serving:
Calories: 577
Fat: 5.9 grams
Protein: 20.5 grams

Sodium: 269 milligrams
Carbohydrates: 111.5 grams
Sugar: 7.8 grams
Fiber: 7.2 grams

Stir-Fry Soup

YIELDS 4 SERVINGS

8 cups purified water

1 cup chopped broccoli spears

1 cup chopped cauliflower

1 cup chopped Vidalia onions

1 cup snow peas

1 cup sliced button mushrooms

1 cup diced red bell peppers

4 garlic cloves, minced

¼ cup low-sodium soy sauce

1. In a large pot, combine all ingredients.

2. Over high heat, bring soup to a boil, reduce heat to a simmer, and cover.

3. Allow soup to simmer for 25 minutes or until all vegetables are softened.

4. Remove from heat and allow to cool.

5. Consume immediately or transfer soup to a large glass container with a tight-fitting lid. Soup can be stored in the refrigerator for up to 5 days or in the freezer for up to 1 month.

Per serving:
Calories: 64
Fat: 0.2 grams
Protein: 4.6 grams

Sodium: 523 milligrams
Carbohydrates: 12.9 grams
Sugar: 6.12
Fiber: 3.9 grams

Black Beans, Tomatoes, and Greens

YIELDS 4 SERVINGS

8 cups purified water

2 (16-ounce) cans no-sodium black beans

4 cups chopped Roma tomatoes

2 cups chopped Vidalia onions

2 cups fresh corn kernels (may also use frozen and thawed)

2 garlic cloves, minced

2 tablespoons ground cumin

2 cups spinach

1. In a large pot, combine all ingredients except spinach.

2. Over high heat, bring soup to a boil, reduce heat to a simmer, and cover.

3. Allow soup to simmer for 25 minutes.

4. Add spinach and stir until leaves are wilted and well combined, about 1–2 minutes.

5. Remove from heat and allow to cool.

6. Consume immediately or transfer soup to a large glass container with a tight-fitting lid. Soup can be stored in the refrigerator for up to 5 days or in the freezer for up to 1 month.

Per serving:
Calories: 343
Fat: 2.3 grams
Protein: 19.7 grams

Sodium: 147 milligrams
Carbohydrates: 65.9 grams
Sugar: 13.5 grams
Fiber: 19.2 grams

Red Cabbage with Greens and Tofu

YIELDS 4 SERVINGS

8 cups purified water

4 cups chopped red cabbage

2 cups chopped kale, ribs removed

3 garlic cloves, minced

1 (16-ounce) package firm tofu, cut into ¼" cubes

3 cups spinach

1. In a large pot, combine water, cabbage, kale, garlic, and tofu.

2. Over high heat, bring soup to a boil, reduce heat to a simmer, and cover.

3. Allow soup to simmer for 20 minutes or until vegetables are softened.

4. Add spinach and stir until leaves are wilted, about 1–2 minutes.

5. Remove from heat and allow to cool.

6. Consume immediately or transfer soup to a large glass container with a tight-fitting lid. Soup can be stored in the refrigerator for up to 5 days or in the freezer for up to 1 month.

Per serving:
Calories: 169
Fat: 5.0 grams
Protein: 16.2 grams

Sodium: 197 milligrams
Carbohydrates: 19.0 grams
Sugar: 4.5 grams
Fiber: 7.1 grams

Roasted Red Pepper with Rosemary

YIELDS 4 SERVINGS

½ cup extra-virgin olive oil, divided

8 red bell peppers, seeded and chopped

4 garlic cloves, chopped

¼ cup dried rosemary

8 cups purified water

1. Preheat oven to 400°F.

2. Prepare a roasting pan or baking sheet by drizzling ¼ cup olive oil to coat evenly. Spread peppers and garlic cloves evenly throughout pan, coat with remaining ¼ cup olive oil, and sprinkle evenly with rosemary.

3. Roast for 40 minutes, turning once after 20 minutes.

4. Transfer peppers, garlic, and bits on pan to a large pot and cover with water.

5. Over high heat, bring soup to a boil, reduce heat to a simmer, and cover.

6. Allow soup to simmer for 20 minutes.

7. Using an immersion blender, submerge blades and blend on high until all ingredients are broken down and thoroughly combined, about 5 minutes.

8. Remove from heat and allow to cool.

9. Consume immediately or transfer soup to a large glass container with a tight-fitting lid. Soup can be stored in the refrigerator for up to 5 days or in the freezer for up to 1 month.

Per serving:
Calories: 218
Fat: 17.9 grams
Protein: 1.8 grams
Sodium: 26 milligrams
Carbohydrates: 12.0 grams
Sugar: 6.3 grams
Fiber: 4.6 grams

Minestrone Soup

YIELDS 4 SERVINGS

4 cups purified water

4 cups puréed tomatoes

2 large potatoes, cut into ¼" cubes

2 carrots, peeled and chopped

2 celery stalks, chopped

1 cup chopped Vidalia onions

4 garlic cloves, minced

2 cups chopped cabbage

1 cup canned red kidney beans (may also use dried beans that have been soaked for 24 hours)

1 cup canned garbanzo beans (may also use dried beans that have been soaked for 24 hours)

2 cups chopped fresh basil

1. In a large pot, combine all ingredients.

2. Over high heat, bring soup to a boil, reduce heat to a simmer, and cover.

3. Allow soup to simmer for 40 minutes or until all vegetables and beans are tender.

4. Remove from heat and allow to cool.

5. Consume immediately or transfer soup to a large glass container with a tight-fitting lid. Soup can be stored in the refrigerator for up to 5 days or in the freezer for up to 1 month.

Per serving:
Calories: 339
Fat: 2.3 grams
Protein: 14.6 grams

Sodium: 452 milligrams
Carbohydrates: 71.3 grams
Sugar: 21.6 grams
Fiber: 15.6 grams

Greens and Acorn Squash

YIELDS 4 SERVINGS

8 cups purified water

4 cups ¼"-cubed acorn squash

2 cups chopped green cabbage

1 tablespoon ground cinnamon

1 tablespoon ground nutmeg

2 cups spinach

1. In a large pot, combine water, squash, cabbage, cinnamon, and nutmeg.

2. Over high heat, bring soup to a boil, reduce heat to a simmer, and cover.

3. Allow soup to simmer for 40 minutes or until squash is fork-tender.

4. Add spinach and stir until leaves are wilted and thoroughly combined, about 1–2 minutes.

5. Remove from heat and allow to cool.

6. Consume immediately or transfer soup to a large glass container with a tight-fitting lid. Soup can be stored in the refrigerator for up to 5 days or in the freezer for up to 1 month.

Per serving:
Calories: 106
Fat: 1.0 grams
Protein: 5.1 grams

Sodium: 121 milligrams
Carbohydrates: 23.8 grams
Sugar: 2.5 grams
Fiber: 7.0 grams

Sweet Potato Split-Pea

YIELDS 4 SERVINGS

8 cups purified water

3 large sweet potatoes, scrubbed and chopped

1 (16-ounce) bag split peas

1 tablespoon ground nutmeg

1. In a large pot, combine all ingredients.

2. Over high heat, bring soup to a boil, reduce heat to a simmer, and cover.

3. Allow soup to simmer for 1 hour, stirring every 5–10 minutes.

4. Remove from heat and allow to cool for 5 minutes.

5. Using an immersion blender, submerge blades and blend on high until all ingredients are broken down and thoroughly combined, about 5 minutes.

6. Consume immediately or transfer soup to a large glass container with a tight-fitting lid. Soup can be stored in the refrigerator for up to 5 days or in the freezer for up to 1 month.

Per serving:
Calories: 512
Fat: 1.6 grams
Protein: 30.1 grams

Sodium: 111 milligrams
Carbohydrates: 96.8 grams
Sugar: 15.3 grams
Fiber: 33.8 grams

CHAPTER 9

Skin-Nourishing Soups

Your exterior complexion is a direct reflection of your interior condition, but few people realize how important the role of diet is in achieving and maintaining healthy skin. Toxicity that wreaks havoc on the cells and systems within the body shows through in the skin's appearance with issues like inflammation, irritation, signs of aging, and even serious conditions like cancers. Fortunately, with the skin-nourishing and cleansing soups found in this chapter, you can achieve a healthy glow and more beautiful appearance. These delicious recipes—including Blueberry-Walnut with Quinoa, Almond-Citrus-Raspberry, Roasted Bell Pepper and Tomato Soup, and Sesame Carrot and Celery—are full of vibrant vegetables, delectable fruits, and other healthful additions like kefir, yogurt, nuts, seeds, nut milks, and even green tea that provide your body with precise combinations of nutrients like vitamins A, Bs, C, and E, as well as minerals like iron, calcium, magnesium, and potassium. In addition, you'll also receive potent antioxidants that combat free-radical damage that could result in skin conditions like blotchiness, wrinkles, and even cancer, and resveratrol, a powerful phytochemical that helps to support the systems responsible for regenerating skin cells, helping to improve the development of collagen and elastin in the skin. So get ready to experience less acne, fewer dark spots, relieved skin conditions, and a minimization of wrinkles as the result of a diet that provides your body with what it needs to purge toxins, replenish skin cells, and rejuvenate the skin!

Blueberry-Walnut with Quinoa

YIELDS 4 SERVINGS

8 cups vanilla almond milk

4 cups blueberries

1 cup walnuts

½ cup ground flaxseed

¼ cup ground chia seeds

2 cups cooked quinoa

1. In a countertop blender, combine almond milk, blueberries, walnuts, flaxseed, and chia seeds.

2. Blend on high until all ingredients are broken down and thoroughly combined, about 2–3 minutes.

3. Add cooked quinoa to soup and stir until thoroughly combined.

4. Consume immediately or transfer soup to a large glass container with a tight-fitting lid and store in the refrigerator for up to 5 days.

QUINOA'S AESTHETIC AMINO ACIDS

Quinoa is one of the few foods that not only packs vitamins, minerals, and phytochemicals into your favorite dishes but also provides every essential and nonessential amino acid. These building blocks of protein improve the body's ability to process and use nutrients and also help support the skin's protein-based structure. With the addition of these amino acids to your daily soup cleanse routine, you also help combat blemishes, wrinkles, and discoloration naturally and easily.

Per serving:
Calories: 670
Fat: 29.7 grams
Protein: 15.6 grams

Sodium: 334 milligrams
Carbohydrates: 85.2 grams
Sugar: 47.5 grams
Fiber: 16.2 grams

Apple-Pear-Grape with Oatmeal and Spice

YIELDS 4 SERVINGS

8 cups vanilla almond milk

2 Fuji apples, peeled, cored, and chopped

2 Bartlett pears, peeled, cored, and chopped

1 cup green seedless grapes

1 cup uncooked oatmeal

1 tablespoon ground cinnamon

1. In a large pot, combine almond milk, apples, pears, grapes, and oatmeal.

2. Over high heat, bring soup to a boil, then reduce heat and simmer for 20 minutes or until fruits are fork-tender.

3. Remove from heat, season with cinnamon, and allow to cool for 30 minutes.

4. Using an immersion blender, submerge blades and blend on high until fruits are broken down, oatmeal is thoroughly combined, and a creamy texture is achieved, about 5 minutes.

5. Consume immediately or transfer soup to a large glass container with a tight-fitting lid and store in the refrigerator for up to 5 days.

GRAPES FOR BEAUTY

One of the best aspects of sweet, delicious grapes is the immense nutrition that's packed into every single serving. One of the most beneficial nutrients of grapes is resveratrol, which can naturally improve your skin's health. Included in skin creams, resveratrol helps combat wrinkles naturally by improving collagen and elastin production and helping maintain the skin's hydration. Packed into your daily soup cleanse routine, grapes can help transform your skin with ease!

Per serving:
Calories: 336
Fat: 6.2 grams
Protein: 5.5 grams

Sodium: 321 milligrams
Carbohydrates: 67.9 grams
Sugar: 49.4 grams
Fiber: 4.5 grams

Pumpkin-Fig-Oat with Cinnamon and Spice

YIELDS 4 SERVINGS

8 cups vanilla almond milk
4 cups ¼"-cubed pumpkin
4 figs, stems removed and chopped
1 cup uncooked oatmeal
¼ cup organic all-natural honey
1 tablespoon ground cinnamon
1 tablespoon ground cardamom
2 teaspoons ground cloves

1. In a large pot, combine all ingredients.

2. Over high heat, bring soup to a boil, then reduce heat and simmer for 30 minutes or until pumpkin is fork-tender.

3. Remove from heat and allow to cool for 30 minutes.

4. Consume immediately or transfer soup to a large glass container with a tight-fitting lid and store in the refrigerator for up to 5 days.

Per serving:
Calories: 407
Fat: 6.5 grams
Protein: 6.7 grams

Sodium: 325 milligrams
Carbohydrates: 86.2 grams
Sugar: 63.4 grams
Fiber: 6.2 grams

Citrus-Fennel

YIELDS 4 SERVINGS

6 cups unsweetened coconut milk
2 oranges, peeled and seeded
2 large pink grapefruits, peeled and seeded
2 cucumbers, ends removed and sliced
1 cup chopped fennel bulb

1. In a countertop blender, combine all ingredients.

2. Blend on high until all ingredients are broken down and thoroughly combined, about 2–3 minutes.

3. Consume immediately or transfer soup to a large glass container with a tight-fitting lid and store in the refrigerator for up to 5 days.

Per serving:
Calories: 163
Fat: 6.2 grams
Protein: 2.0 grams

Sodium: 66 milligrams
Carbohydrates: 23.8 grams
Sugar: 15.0 grams
Fiber: 3.1 grams

Berry-Quinoa with Almonds and Flax

YIELDS 4 SERVINGS

7 cups vanilla almond milk

2 cups raw almonds

2 cups strawberries, tops removed

2 cups blueberries

½ cup ground flaxseed

2 tablespoons organic honey

1 tablespoon ground cinnamon

2 cups cooked quinoa

1. In a countertop blender, combine almond milk and almonds.

2. Blend on high until almonds are broken down and thoroughly combined, about 2–3 minutes.

3. Add strawberries, blueberries, flaxseed, honey, and cinnamon to the blender and blend on high until all ingredients are broken down and thoroughly combined, about 2–3 minutes.

4. Add quinoa to the soup and stir until thoroughly combined.

5. Consume immediately or transfer soup to a large glass container with a tight-fitting lid and store in the refrigerator for up to 5 days.

OMEGA-PACKED FLAXSEED

By adding a scoop of ground flaxseed to your favorite soups, you can improve the nutrition and health benefits of your soup cleanse simply and easily. Omega-3, -6, and -9 fatty acids act as powerful antioxidants that fight free-radical damage in the skin's layers, helping to combat wrinkles, blemishes, and even cancerous changes!

Per serving:
Calories: 856
Fat: 48.6 grams
Protein: 24.2 grams

Sodium: 292 milligrams
Carbohydrates: 92.3 grams
Sugar: 51.8 grams
Fiber: 19.3 grams

Lemon-Herb Salmon Soup

YIELDS 4 SERVINGS

4 tablespoons coconut oil, divided
1 pound salmon fillets, cleaned
1 cup lemon juice
¼ cup chopped fresh basil, divided
¼ cup chopped fresh rosemary, divided
4 lemons, sliced, divided
8 cups purified water

1. Preheat oven to 400°F.

2. Drizzle 2 tablespoons coconut oil evenly over a baking sheet or roasting pan. Place the salmon on the prepared pan, drizzle with 1 tablespoon coconut oil, pour lemon juice over salmon, sprinkle ⅛ cup each of the basil and rosemary, and top with half of the lemon slices. Bake for 15 minutes.

3. Flip the fish over, drizzle with the remaining 1 tablespoon coconut oil, sprinkle the remaining ⅛ cup each of basil and rosemary, and top with remaining lemon slices. Continue baking for 15–20 minutes or until salmon is cooked through.

4. Pour salmon, herbs, lemon slices, and juices into a large pot. Add water and bring to a boil over high heat. Reduce heat to a simmer and simmer for 10 minutes.

5. Consume immediately or transfer soup to a large glass container with a tight-fitting lid and store in the refrigerator for up to 5 days.

COCONUT OIL'S MCFAS

Coconut oil has one distinct quality that sets it apart from every other oil: medium-chain fatty acids (MCFAs). Helping to fight free-radical damage, support protein absorption and utilization, and promote the production and retention of collagen and elastin, these MCFAs not only improve the health of the skin but also make it appear healthier with a glow, fewer wrinkles, reduced discoloration, and improved elasticity! In addition to the plentiful aesthetic benefits, MCFAs also help improve digestion, metabolism, and the body's use of nutrients for a more effective cleansing process that boosts the body's health in almost every aspect.

Per serving:
Calories: 261
Fat: 14.7 grams
Protein: 23.2 grams

Sodium: 71 milligrams
Carbohydrates: 8.9 grams
Sugar: 2.2 grams
Fiber: 2.4 grams

Pomegranate with Lemon and Avocado

YIELDS 4 SERVINGS

8 cups purified water

3 cups pomegranate jewels

½ cup freshly squeezed lemon juice

4 Hass avocados, peeled and seeded

½ cup ground flaxseed

1. In a countertop blender, combine all ingredients.

2. Blend on high until all ingredients are broken down and thoroughly combined, about 2–3 minutes.

3. Consume immediately or transfer soup to a large glass container with a tight-fitting lid and store in the refrigerator for up to 5 days.

Per serving:
Calories: 439
Fat: 28.1 grams
Protein: 7.2 grams

Sodium: 39 milligrams
Carbohydrates: 43.1 grams
Sugar: 19.2 grams
Fiber: 19.5 grams

Almond-Citrus-Raspberry

YIELDS 4 SERVINGS

6 cups purified water

2 cups freshly squeezed orange juice

2 cups raw almonds

½ cup ground flaxseed

2 oranges, peeled and seeded

2 kiwis, peeled and halved

2 cups raspberries

1. In a countertop blender, combine water, orange juice, almonds, and flaxseed and blend on high until almonds are broken down and all ingredients are thoroughly combined, about 2–3 minutes.

2. Add oranges, kiwis, and raspberries and blend on high until all ingredients are broken down and thoroughly combined, about 2–3 minutes.

3. Consume immediately or transfer soup to a large glass container with a tight-fitting lid and store in the refrigerator for up to 5 days.

Per serving:
Calories: 627
Fat: 42.8 grams
Protein: 19.7 grams

Sodium: 21 milligrams
Carbohydrates: 51.5 grams
Sugar: 26.1 grams
Fiber: 19.4 grams

Sesame-Soy Stir-Fry Soup

YIELDS 4 SERVINGS

4 tablespoons sesame oil

½ cup low-sodium soy sauce

1 cup chopped red bell peppers

1 cup chopped green bell peppers

1 red onion, chopped

1 cup broccoli florets

1 cup chopped snow peas

8 cups purified water

1. In a large pot over high heat, heat oil for 2–3 minutes or until fragrant. Reduce heat to medium-high.

2. Add soy sauce, bell peppers, onion, broccoli, and snow peas. Stirring regularly, sauté for 10–15 minutes or until vegetables are tender.

3. Add water, bring to a simmer, and simmer for 15 minutes.

4. Consume immediately or transfer soup to a large glass container with a tight-fitting lid and store in the refrigerator for up to 5 days.

Per serving:
Calories: 179
Fat: 13.2 grams
Protein: 4.9 grams

Sodium: 1174 milligrams
Carbohydrates: 10.5 grams
Sugar: 4.5 grams
Fiber: 2.6 grams

Sweet Potato and Black Bean with Red Onion

YIELDS 4 SERVINGS

6 cups unsweetened almond milk

2 large sweet potatoes, cubed into ¼" pieces

2 cups minced red onion

1 (16-ounce) can no-sodium black beans

2 cups Greek yogurt

1. In a large pot, combine the almond milk, sweet potatoes, red onion, and black beans. Bring to a boil over high heat. Reduce heat and simmer for 20 minutes or until sweet potatoes are softened.

2. Remove from heat and cool for 30 minutes.

3. Stir in Greek yogurt.

4. Consume immediately or transfer soup to a large glass container with a tight-fitting lid and store in the refrigerator for up to 5 days.

Per serving:
Calories: 304
Fat: 9.2 grams
Protein: 17.8 grams

Sodium: 320 milligrams
Carbohydrates: 37.0 grams
Sugar: 9.6 grams
Fiber: 8.5 grams

Roasted Bell Pepper and Tomato Soup

YIELDS 4 SERVINGS

4 tablespoons extra-virgin olive oil, divided

4 red bell peppers, chopped

4 green tomatoes, chopped

6 garlic cloves, minced

8 cups purified water

4 cups chopped spinach

1. Preheat oven to 400°F.

2. Prepare a baking sheet or roasting pan by drizzling with 2 tablespoons olive oil to coat evenly. Spread the bell peppers and tomatoes evenly throughout the pan, drizzle remaining 2 tablespoons olive oil over the vegetables, and roast for 45 minutes, turning the vegetables after 20 minutes.

3. Pour all roasted vegetables into a large pot and add the garlic and water.

4. Bring soup to a boil, reduce heat to a simmer, and simmer for 20 minutes.

5. Add spinach to the soup, stirring for 5 minutes or until spinach is wilted.

6. Consume immediately or transfer soup to a large glass container with a tight-fitting lid and store in the refrigerator for up to 5 days.

Per serving:
Calories: 137
Fat: 6.9 grams
Protein: 3.8 grams

Sodium: 63 milligrams
Carbohydrates: 16.0 grams
Sugar: 10.1 grams
Fiber: 4.6 grams

Kale-Apple-Berries

8 cups purified water

2 large kale leaves, ribs removed

4 Fuji apples, peeled and cored

1 cup raspberries

1 cup strawberries, tops removed

1 tablespoon ground cardamom

1" piece of ginger, peeled and sliced

1. In a countertop blender, combine all ingredients.

2. Blend on high until all ingredients are broken down and thoroughly combined, about 2–3 minutes.

3. Consume immediately or transfer soup to a large glass container with a tight-fitting lid and store in the refrigerator for up to 5 days.

Per serving:

Calories: 109

Fat: 0.3 grams

Protein: 1.3 grams

Sodium: 19 milligrams

Carbohydrates: 28.2 grams

Sugar: 19.4 grams

Fiber: 5.3 grams

Beets, Greens, and Nectarines

8 cups purified water

2 red beets, roasted and chopped

4 nectarines, pitted

2 cups spinach

1 teaspoon ground nutmeg

1. In a countertop blender, combine all ingredients.

2. Blend on high until all ingredients are broken down and thoroughly combined, about 2–3 minutes.

3. Consume immediately or transfer soup to a large glass container with a tight-fitting lid and store in the refrigerator for up to 5 days.

Per serving:

Calories: 85

Fat: 0.5 grams

Protein: 2.6 grams

Sodium: 62 milligrams

Carbohydrates: 19.7 grams

Sugar: 14.1 grams

Fiber: 4.0 grams

Sweet Berries with Squash and Sweet Potato

YIELDS 4 SERVINGS

6 cups vanilla almond milk

2 cups cubed acorn squash

2 medium sweet potatoes, cubed

2 cups vanilla kefir

2 cups blackberries

1. In a large pot over high heat, bring the almond milk, squash, and sweet potatoes to a boil.

2. Reduce heat to a simmer and simmer for 30 minutes or until squash and sweet potatoes are fork-tender.

3. Remove soup from heat and allow to cool for 15 minutes. Using an immersion blender, submerge blades and blend on high until ingredients are broken down and thoroughly combined, about 5 minutes.

4. Add the kefir and blackberries to the soup and stir well until all ingredients are thoroughly combined.

5. Consume immediately or transfer soup to a large glass container with a tight-fitting lid and store in the refrigerator for up to 5 days.

Per serving:
Calories: 329
Fat: 6.1 grams
Protein: 8.1 grams

Sodium: 320 milligrams
Carbohydrates: 64.3 grams
Sugar: 41.7 grams
Fiber: 7.7 grams

Waldorf Chicken Salad Soup

YIELDS 4 SERVINGS

4 cups unsweetened almond milk

2 cups vanilla kefir

2 cups Greek yogurt

1 tablespoon garlic powder

1 tablespoon onion powder

2 cups chopped cooked chicken

1 cup chopped celery

1 cup chopped red cabbage

2 cups sliced red grapes

1. Combine the almond milk, kefir, Greek yogurt, garlic powder, and onion powder in a blender and blend on high until ingredients are thoroughly combined, about 1 minute.

2. Transfer the blender's contents to a large glass container with a tight-fitting lid.

3. Stir in the chicken, celery, cabbage, and grapes until all ingredients are thoroughly combined, about 1 minute.

4. Consume immediately or store in the refrigerator for up to 5 days.

Per serving:
Calories: 398
Fat: 13.7 grams
Protein: 33.1 grams

Sodium: 320 milligrams
Carbohydrates: 36.2 grams
Sugar: 28.6 grams
Fiber: 3.0 grams

Sweet and Spicy Spinach, Fig, and Chicken

YIELDS 4 SERVINGS

6 cups vanilla almond milk

6 figs, stems removed

½" piece of ginger, peeled and sliced

2 cups Greek yogurt

2 cups chopped spinach

2 cups chopped cooked chicken

1. In a countertop blender, combine almond milk, figs, and ginger and blend on high until all ingredients are broken down and thoroughly combined, about 2–3 minutes.

2. Transfer soup to a large glass container and stir in the Greek yogurt, spinach, and chicken until all ingredients are well blended.

3. Consume immediately or transfer soup to a large glass container with a tight-fitting lid and store in the refrigerator for up to 5 days.

Per serving:
Calories: 421
Fat: 31.1 grams
Protein: 29.2 grams

Sodium: 340 milligrams
Carbohydrates: 47.0 grams
Sugar: 43.7 grams
Fiber: 3.1 grams

Sesame Carrot and Celery

YIELDS 4 SERVINGS

4 tablespoons sesame oil, divided

4 carrots, peeled and chopped

4 celery stalks, chopped

6 cups vanilla almond milk

2 cups Greek yogurt

1. Preheat oven to 400°F.

2. Prepare a baking sheet or roasting pan by drizzling with 2 tablespoons sesame oil to coat evenly. Spread the carrots and celery evenly throughout the pan, drizzle remaining 2 tablespoons sesame oil over the vegetables, and roast for 45 minutes, turning the vegetables after 20 minutes.

3. Remove from heat, and cool for 45 minutes.

4. Pour the roasted vegetables and drippings into a blender and add the almond milk and Greek yogurt.

5. Blend on high until all ingredients are broken down and well blended, about 2–3 minutes.

6. Consume immediately or transfer soup to a large glass container with a tight-fitting lid and store in the refrigerator for up to 5 days.

Per serving:

Calories: 336

Fat: 17.0 grams

Protein: 11.3 grams

Sodium: 349 milligrams

Carbohydrates: 35.0 grams

Sugar: 31.4 grams

Fiber: 2.4 grams

Roasted Carrot with Three Oils

YIELDS 4 SERVINGS

2 tablespoons sesame oil, divided

2 tablespoons extra-virgin olive oil, divided

2 tablespoons coconut oil, divided

8 carrots, peeled and chopped

6 cups vanilla almond milk

2 cups Greek yogurt

1. Preheat oven to 400°F.

2. Prepare a baking sheet or roasting pan by drizzling with 1 tablespoon of each of the oils to coat the pan evenly. Spread the carrots evenly throughout the pan, drizzle remaining 1 tablespoon of each oil over the carrots, and roast for 40 minutes, turning the carrots after 20 minutes.

3. Remove from heat and cool for 45 minutes.

4. Pour the roasted carrots and drippings into a blender and add the almond milk and Greek yogurt.

5. Blend on high until all ingredients are broken down and well blended, about 1–2 minutes.

6. Consume immediately or transfer soup to a large glass container with a tight-fitting lid and store in the refrigerator for up to 5 days.

Per serving:
Calories: 391
Fat: 21.1 grams
Protein: 11.6 grams

Sodium: 359 milligrams
Carbohydrates: 39.7 grams
Sugar: 33.8 grams
Fiber: 3.4 grams

Garlicky Roasted Red Pepper, Eggplant, and Herb

YIELDS 4 SERVINGS

4 tablespoons extra-virgin olive oil, divided

4 red bell peppers, cut into ¼" strips

2 small eggplants, cut into ¼" cubes

6 garlic cloves, minced

2 tablespoons dried basil

2 tablespoons dried rosemary

2 tablespoons dried oregano

8 cups Roasted Red Vegetable Broth (see Chapter 10)

1. Preheat oven to 400°F.

2. Prepare a baking sheet or roasting pan by drizzling with 2 tablespoons olive oil to coat evenly. Spread the bell pepper and eggplant evenly throughout the pan, drizzle remaining 2 tablespoons oil over the vegetables, and sprinkle minced garlic, basil, rosemary, and oregano to coat. Roast for 40 minutes, turning the vegetables after 20 minutes.

3. Remove from heat, transfer the roasted vegetables and drippings into a large pot, and add the broth.

4. Bring to a boil over high heat and reduce heat to a simmer. Simmer for 10 minutes and remove from heat.

5. Consume immediately or transfer soup to a large glass container with a tight-fitting lid and store in the refrigerator for up to 5 days.

Per serving:
Calories: 238
Fat: 13.9 grams
Protein: 7.1 grams

Sodium: 64 milligrams
Carbohydrates: 25.0 grams
Sugar: 12.1 grams
Fiber: 12.0 grams

Herbed Acorn Squash

4 tablespoons coconut oil, divided

3 cups peeled, seeded, and chopped acorn squash

2 cups chopped fresh sage

6 cups almond milk

2 cups Greek yogurt

1. Preheat oven to 400°F.

2. Prepare a baking sheet or roasting pan by drizzling with 2 tablespoons coconut oil to coat the pan evenly. Spread the acorn squash evenly throughout the pan, drizzle remaining coconut oil over the squash, sprinkle with the sage to coat, and roast for 40 minutes. Turn the squash after 20 minutes to ensure even roasting.

3. Remove from heat and cool for 45 minutes.

4. Pour the roasted squash and drippings into a blender and add the almond milk and Greek yogurt.

5. Blend on high until all ingredients are broken down and well-blended, about 3–5 minutes.

6. Consume immediately or transfer soup to a large glass container with a tight-fitting lid and store in the refrigerator for up to 5 days.

Per serving:
Calories: 333
Fat: 15.3 grams
Protein: 11.3 grams

Sodium: 278 milligrams
Carbohydrates: 35.0 grams
Sugar: 14.5 grams
Fiber: 9.5 grams

Pear-Apple-Cucumber Cream

4 cups vanilla almond milk

2 cups kefir

2 cups Greek yogurt

2 Bartlett pears, peeled and cored

2 Granny Smith apples, peeled and cored

2 cucumbers, peeled with ends removed

½" piece of ginger, peeled and sliced

1 tablespoon ground cinnamon

2 teaspoons ground cloves

1. In a countertop blender, combine all ingredients.

2. Blend on high until all ingredients are broken down and thoroughly combined, about 3–5 minutes.

3. Consume immediately or transfer soup to a large glass container with a tight-fitting lid and store in the refrigerator for up to 5 days.

Per serving:
Calories: 379
Fat: 11.7 grams
Protein: 15.3 grams

Sodium: 263 milligrams
Carbohydrates: 55.5 grams
Sugar: 44.2 grams
Fiber: 7.4 grams

CHAPTER 10

Bone Broths

Few people realize the vast number of health benefits that can be gained simply by enjoying bowls of bone-broth-based soup. When the cartilage and bones of animals are boiled and reduced, the result is a delicious and unique concoction that contains vitamins A, Bs, C, and E, and minerals like calcium, magnesium, and iron. Bone broths also have unique nutrients like amino acids, silica, gelatin, glucosamine, and chondroitin. Together, these vitamins, minerals, and nutrients work to improve the condition of your hair, skin, and nails; reduce inflammation; improve bone health; support nervous system functioning; and even improve blood health. All of these benefits can be realized by simply following easy "set it and forget it" recipes like Lemon-Basil Chicken Broth, Tarragon Turkey Broth, and Thanksgiving Turkey Broth that can be stored or saved, included in your favorite soups, and used to enhance the already nutritious and delicious soup recipes you enjoy in your daily soup-cleansing routine. Rather than using water or store-bought broths, you can create delicious and superiorly nutritious bone broths that not only far surpass store-bought varieties in flavor but in nutritional content as well. Enjoy!

NUTRITIONAL ANALYSIS FOR BROTHS

Note: Many things, including cooking time, can impact the nutritional composition of broths. As the veggies, meat, and bones are removed, some, but not all of the nutrients are left behind. The nutrition stats in this section are best estimates based on the ingredients used, but be aware that there may be some differences in the nutritional value of the broth you make in your own home.

Tarragon Turkey Broth

YIELDS 16 CUPS OR 8 SERVINGS

16 cups purified water
1 turkey carcass, meat removed
2 yellow onions, peeled and chopped
4 tablespoons dried tarragon
4 garlic cloves
2 cups shredded cooked turkey

1. Combine all ingredients in a large pot over high heat.

2. Bring soup to a boil, reduce heat to a simmer, and cover.

3. Allow soup to simmer for 1–4 hours.

4. Remove from heat and allow to cool.

5. Strain bones, vegetables, and solids from the soup by placing a strainer over a large pot and discard solids.

6. Consume immediately or transfer soup to a large glass container with a tight-fitting lid. Soup can be stored in the refrigerator for up to 5 days or in the freezer for up to 1 month.

HOLIDAY LEFTOVERS MAKE FOR PERFECT BONE BROTH BASES

When the holidays are over and you find yourself with a turkey carcass, you can use the turkey's seemingly useless skeleton to create and freeze delicious and nutritious bone broths that pack tons of flavor and valuable nutrients into your favorite soup recipes. By creating your own homemade bone broths, you can control the ingredients and flavors, while ensuring that your broths are free of the unhealthy preservatives and additives that make the store-bought broths unhealthy options.

Per serving:
Calories: 40
Fat: 1.2 grams
Protein: 3.6 grams
Sodium: 46 milligrams
Carbohydrates: 3.6 grams
Sugar: 2.0 grams
Fiber: 0.8 grams

Mushroom Beef Broth

YIELDS 16 CUPS OR 8 SERVINGS

4 tablespoons extra-virgin olive oil, divided

3 pounds beef bones (ribs, neck, etc.), meat removed

16 cups purified water

2 yellow onions, peeled and chopped

1 pound cremini mushrooms

4 garlic cloves

1. Preheat oven to 400°F.

2. Evenly coat a large roasting pan or baking sheet with 2 tablespoons olive oil. Place the bones on the pan and drizzle with the remaining 2 tablespoons olive oil. Roast for 45 minutes, turning once after 20–25 minutes.

3. Pour bones and drippings into a large pot and add water and all additional ingredients.

4. Over high heat, bring soup to a boil, reduce heat to a simmer, and cover.

5. Allow soup to simmer for 4–24 hours.

6. Remove from heat and allow to cool.

7. Strain bones, vegetables, and solids from the soup by placing a strainer over a large pot. Discard solids.

8. Consume immediately or transfer soup to a large glass container with a tight-fitting lid. Soup can be stored in the refrigerator for up to 5 days or in the freezer for up to 1 month.

Per serving:
Calories: 84
Fat: 5.1 grams
Protein: 5.2 grams

Sodium: 78 milligrams
Carbohydrates: 4.2 grams
Sugar: 2.8 grams
Fiber: 0.8 grams

Best Beef Broth

YIELDS 16 CUPS OR 8 SERVINGS

4 tablespoons extra-virgin olive oil, divided

3 pounds beef bones (ribs, neck, etc.), meat removed

16 cups purified water

2 yellow onions, peeled and chopped

2 carrots, peeled, tops removed, and roughly chopped

4 celery ribs, leaves intact

4 garlic cloves

1. Preheat oven to 400°F.

2. Evenly coat a large roasting pan or baking sheet with 2 tablespoons olive oil. Place the bones on the pan and drizzle with the remaining 2 tablespoons olive oil; roast for 45 minutes, turning once after 20–25 minutes.

3. Pour bones and drippings into a large pot and add water and all additional ingredients.

4. Over high heat, bring soup to a boil, reduce heat to a simmer, and cover.

5. Allow soup to simmer for 4–24 hours.

6. Remove from heat and allow to cool.

7. Strain bones, vegetables, and solids from the soup by placing a strainer over a large pot. Discard solids.

8. Consume immediately or transfer soup to a large glass container with a tight-fitting lid. Soup can be stored in the refrigerator for up to 5 days or in the freezer for up to 1 month.

Per serving:
Calories: 79
Fat: 5.0 grams
Protein: 4.0 grams

Sodium: 102 milligrams
Carbohydrates: 4.4 grams
Sugar: 2.6 grams
Fiber: 0.8 grams

Herbed Vegetable Beef Broth

YIELDS 16 CUPS OR 8 SERVINGS

4 tablespoons extra-virgin olive oil, divided

3 pounds beef bones (ribs, neck, etc.), meat removed

1 tablespoon dried sage

1 tablespoon dried thyme

1 tablespoon dried oregano

16 cups purified water

1 yellow onion, peeled and chopped

1 red onion, peeled and chopped

1 pound portobello mushrooms

4 garlic cloves

1. Preheat oven to 400°F.

2. Evenly coat a large roasting pan or baking sheet with 2 tablespoons olive oil. Place the bones on the pan and drizzle with the remaining 2 tablespoons olive oil. Coat evenly with sage, thyme, and oregano. Roast for 45 minutes, turning once after 20–25 minutes.

3. Pour bones and drippings into a large pot and add water and all additional ingredients.

4. Over high heat, bring soup to a boil, reduce heat to a simmer, and cover.

5. Allow soup to simmer for 4–24 hours.

6. Remove from heat and allow to cool.

7. Strain bones, vegetables, and solids from the soup by placing a strainer over a large pot. Discard solids.

8. Consume immediately or transfer soup to a large glass container with a tight-fitting lid. Soup can be stored in the refrigerator for up to 5 days or in the freezer for up to 1 month.

Per serving:

Calories: 69

Fat: 5.0 grams

Protein: 3.6 grams

Sodium: 74 milligrams

Carbohydrates: 2.3 grams

Sugar: 1.5 grams

Fiber: 0.8 grams

Peppered Beef Broth

YIELDS 16 CUPS OR 8 SERVINGS

4 tablespoons extra-virgin olive oil, divided

3 pounds beef bones (ribs, neck, etc.), meat removed

2 yellow onions, peeled and chopped

2 red bell peppers, stems and seeds removed and chopped

2 green bell peppers, stems and seeds removed and chopped

2 poblano peppers, stems and seeds removed and chopped

4 garlic cloves

16 cups purified water

1. Preheat oven to 400°F.

2. Evenly coat a large roasting pan or baking sheet with 2 tablespoons olive oil. Place the bones, onions, peppers, and garlic cloves on the pan and drizzle with the remaining 2 tablespoons olive oil. Roast for 45 minutes, turning once after 20–25 minutes.

3. Pour bones, onions, garlic cloves, drippings, and water into a large pot.

4. Over high heat, bring soup to a boil, reduce heat to a simmer, and cover.

5. Allow soup to simmer for 4–24 hours.

6. Remove from heat and allow to cool.

7. Strain bones, vegetables, and solids from the soup by placing a strainer over a large pot. Discard solids.

8. Consume immediately or transfer soup to a large glass container with a tight-fitting lid. Soup can be stored in the refrigerator for up to 5 days or in the freezer for up to 1 month.

GARLIC'S POTENT PHYTOCHEMICAL

The garlic clove is home to one of the most impressive phytochemicals around: allicin. With a healthy dose of allicin, you can look forward to better blood and heart health, improved memory and cognition, and reduced chances of developing serious degenerative diseases of the mind like Alzheimer's disease. While research is still being conducted on the many benefits of garlic's potent phytochemical, this delicious and nutritious bone broth recipe contains a healthy dose of garlic that may help improve your health long after your soup cleanse is done.

Per serving:
Calories: 75
Fat: 5.1 grams
Protein: 3.9 grams

Sodium: 61 milligrams
Carbohydrates: 3.3 grams
Sugar: 0.4 grams
Fiber: 1.1 grams

French Onion Beef Broth

YIELDS 16 CUPS OR 8 SERVINGS

4 tablespoons extra-virgin olive oil, divided

3 pounds beef bones (ribs, neck, etc.), meat removed

6 yellow onions, peeled and chopped

4 garlic cloves

2 tablespoons dried thyme

¼ cup red wine vinegar

16 cups purified water

1. Preheat oven to 400°F.

2. Evenly coat a large roasting pan or baking sheet with 2 tablespoons olive oil. Place the bones, onions, and garlic cloves on the pan and drizzle with the remaining 2 tablespoons olive oil; coat with dried thyme. Roast for 45 minutes, turning once after 20–25 minutes.

3. Pour bones, onions, garlic cloves, and drippings into a large pot and add vinegar and water.

4. Over high heat, bring soup to a boil, reduce heat to a simmer, and cover.

5. Allow soup to simmer for 4–24 hours.

6. Remove from heat and allow to cool.

7. Strain bones, vegetables, and solids from the soup by placing a strainer over a large pot. Discard solids.

8. Consume immediately or transfer soup to a large glass container with a tight-fitting lid. Soup can be stored in the refrigerator for up to 5 days or in the freezer for up to 1 month.

Per serving:
Calories: 74
Fat: 5.0 grams
Protein: 5.4 grams

Sodium: 79 milligrams
Carbohydrates: 1.9 grams
Sugar: 0.7 grams
Fiber: 0.4 grams

Garlic-Vegetable Beef Broth

YIELDS 16 CUPS OR 8 SERVINGS

4 tablespoons extra-virgin olive oil, divided

3 pounds beef bones (ribs, neck, etc.), meat removed

2 yellow onions, peeled and chopped

4 carrots, peeled and chopped

4 celery ribs, chopped

10 garlic cloves

16 cups purified water

1. Preheat oven to 400°F.

2. Evenly coat a large roasting pan or baking sheet with 2 tablespoons olive oil. Place the bones, onions, carrots, celery, and garlic cloves on the pan and drizzle with the remaining 2 tablespoons olive oil. Roast for 45 minutes, turning once after 20–25 minutes.

3. Pour bones, vegetables, garlic cloves, and drippings into a large pot and add water.

4. Over high heat, bring soup to a boil, reduce heat to a simmer, and cover.

5. Allow soup to simmer for 4–24 hours.

6. Remove from heat and allow to cool.

7. Strain bones, vegetables, and solids from the soup by placing a strainer over a large pot. Discard solids.

8. Consume immediately or transfer soup to a large glass container with a tight-fitting lid. Soup can be stored in the refrigerator for up to 5 days or in the freezer for up to 1 month.

Per serving:
Calories: 74
Fat: 5.1 grams
Protein: 4.6 grams
Sodium: 64 milligrams
Carbohydrates: 2.3 grams
Sugar: 0.6 grams
Fiber: 0.5 grams

Lemon-Tarragon Chicken Broth

YIELDS 16 CUPS

16 cups purified water

2 tablespoons extra-virgin olive oil

1 large chicken carcass

1 yellow onion, peeled and chopped

2 tablespoons dried tarragon

4 garlic cloves

¼ cup freshly squeezed lemon juice

1. Add water, olive oil, chicken carcass bones, onions, tarragon, and garlic cloves to a large pot.

2. Over high heat, bring soup to a boil, reduce heat to a simmer, and cover.

3. Allow soup to simmer for 4–24 hours.

4. Remove from heat, add lemon juice, cover, and allow to cool.

5. Strain bones, vegetables, and solids from the soup by placing a strainer over a large pot. Discard solids.

6. Consume immediately or transfer soup to a large glass container with a tight-fitting lid. Soup can be stored in the refrigerator for up to 5 days or in the freezer for up to 1 month.

LEMON'S HEALTH-BOOSTING PROPERTIES

Tart and acidic, the juice of a lemon has a very distinct taste . . . and has some health benefits few people are aware of. The health benefits of lemon juice include improved digestion, cardiovascular benefits, and even aesthetic improvements to the skin, hair, and nails. Add to these benefits the fact that lemon juice can help the immune system fend off bacterial and viral infections, and you can clearly see that this juice that makes everyone pucker up is an essential for improving health as well!

Per serving:
Calories: 47
Fat: 4.9 grams
Protein: 3.5 grams

Sodium: 62 milligrams
Carbohydrates: 2.0 grams
Sugar: 0.5 grams
Fiber: 0.1 grams

Curried Vegetable Chicken Broth

YIELDS 16 CUPS

1 large chicken carcass
2 tablespoons extra-virgin olive oil
2 yellow onions, peeled and chopped
3 carrots, peeled and chopped
4 celery ribs, leaves intact
4 garlic cloves
2 tablespoons dried thyme
2 tablespoons curry powder
1 teaspoon ground nutmeg
16 cups purified water

1. In a large pot, combine chicken carcass bones, olive oil, vegetables, garlic, spices, and water.

2. Over high heat, bring soup to a boil, reduce heat to a simmer, and cover.

3. Allow soup to simmer for 4–24 hours.

4. Remove from heat and allow to cool.

5. Strain bones, vegetables, and solids from the soup by placing a strainer over a large pot. Discard solids.

6. Consume immediately or transfer soup to a large glass container with a tight-fitting lid. Soup can be stored in the refrigerator for up to 5 days or in the freezer for up to 1 month.

Per serving:
Calories: 75
Fat: 5.3 grams
Protein: 4.4 grams

Sodium: 58 milligrams
Carbohydrates: 2.4 grams
Sugar: 0.4 grams
Fiber: 1.3 grams

Sweet and Spicy Chicken Broth

YIELDS 16 CUPS OR 8 SERVINGS

1 large chicken carcass

2 tablespoons extra-virgin olive oil

1 yellow onion, peeled and chopped

4 figs, chopped

2 apples, peeled, cored, and chopped

1 Bartlett pear, peeled, cored, and chopped

4 celery ribs, leaves intact

4" piece of ginger, peeled and sliced

1 teaspoon ground cinnamon

16 cups purified water

1. In a large pot, combine chicken carcass, olive oil, onion, fruits, celery, ginger, cinnamon, and water.

2. Over high heat, bring soup to a boil, reduce heat to a simmer, and cover.

3. Allow soup to simmer for 4–24 hours.

4. Remove from heat and allow to cool.

5. Strain bones, fruits, and solids from the soup by placing a strainer over a large pot. Discard solids.

6. Consume immediately or transfer soup to a large glass container with a tight-fitting lid. Soup can be stored in the refrigerator for up to 5 days or in the freezer for up to 1 month.

Per serving:
Calories: 77
Fat: 5.0 grams
Protein: 3.9 grams

Sodium: 61 milligrams
Carbohydrates: 4.2 grams
Sugar: 2.8 grams
Fiber: 0.8 grams

Lemon-Basil Chicken Broth

YIELDS 16 CUPS OR 8 SERVINGS

16 cups purified water

1 large chicken carcass

4 garlic cloves, chopped

4 cups freshly squeezed lemon juice

½ cup chopped dried sage

3 cups chopped dried basil

1. In a large pot, combine all ingredients.

2. Over high heat, bring soup to a boil, reduce heat to a simmer, and cover.

3. Allow soup to simmer for 4–24 hours.

4. Remove from heat and allow to cool.

5. Strain bones and solids from the soup by placing a strainer over a large pot. Discard solids.

6. Consume immediately or transfer soup to a large glass container with a tight-fitting lid. Soup can be stored in the refrigerator for up to 5 days or in the freezer for up to 1 month.

Per serving:
Calories: 73
Fat: 2.2 grams
Protein: 3.7 grams

Sodium: 64 milligrams
Carbohydrates: 9.7 grams
Sugar: 3.1 grams
Fiber: 0.8 grams

Mediterranean Chicken Broth

YIELDS 16 CUPS OR 8 SERVINGS

4 tablespoons extra-virgin olive oil, divided

1 large chicken carcass

2 cups chopped red onions

4 garlic cloves, chopped

4 tomatoes, chopped

1 large artichoke, chopped

½ cup chopped dried sage

½ cup chopped dried basil

16 cups purified water

1. Preheat oven to 400°F.

2. Evenly coat a large roasting pan or baking sheet with 2 tablespoons olive oil. Place carcass, onions, garlic, tomatoes, and artichokes on pan and season with sage and basil; drizzle with remaining 2 tablespoons olive oil.

3. Roast vegetables for 40 minutes, turning after 20 minutes.

4. Transfer carcass, vegetables, and drippings from pan to a large pot and cover with water.

5. Over high heat, bring soup to a boil, reduce heat to a simmer, and cover.

6. Allow soup to simmer for 4–24 hours.

7. Remove from heat and allow to cool.

8. Strain bones, vegetables, and solids from the soup by placing a strainer over a large pot. Discard solids.

9. Consume immediately or transfer soup to a large glass container with a tight-fitting lid. Soup can be stored in the refrigerator for up to 5 days or in the freezer for up to 1 month.

Per serving:
Calories: 78
Fat: 5.0 grams
Protein: 4.5 grams

Sodium: 72 milligrams
Carbohydrates: 3.7 grams
Sugar: 1.7 grams
Fiber: 1.9 grams

Traditional Vegetable-Based Chicken Broth

YIELDS 16 CUPS OR 8 SERVINGS

16 cups purified water

1 large chicken carcass

10 garlic cloves, chopped

2 large red onions, peeled and chopped

2 Vidalia onions, peeled and chopped

4 carrots, peeled, tops removed, and chopped

6 celery ribs, chopped

½ cup chopped dried basil

½ cup chopped dried sage

1. In a large pot, combine all ingredients.

2. Over high heat, bring soup to a boil, reduce heat to a simmer, and cover.

3. Allow soup to simmer for 4–24 hours.

4. Remove from heat and allow to cool.

5. Strain bones, and solids from the soup by placing a strainer over a large pot. Discard solids.

6. Consume immediately or transfer soup to a large glass container with a tight-fitting lid. Soup can be stored in the refrigerator for up to 5 days or in the freezer for up to 1 month.

Per serving:
Calories: 45
Fat: 1.6 grams
Protein: 3.0 grams

Sodium: 55 milligrams
Carbohydrates: 4.7 grams
Sugar: 2.3 grams
Fiber: 0.6 grams

Italian Wedding Chicken Broth

YIELDS 16 CUPS OR 8 SERVINGS

16 cups purified water

1 large chicken carcass

4 garlic cloves, chopped

4 cups freshly squeezed lemon juice

1 tablespoon roughly chopped caraway seeds

½ cup chopped dried sage

½ cup chopped dried basil

1. In a large pot, combine all ingredients.

2. Over high heat, bring soup to a boil, reduce heat to a simmer, and cover.

3. Allow soup to simmer for 4–24 hours.

4. Remove from heat and allow to cool.

5. Strain bones and solids from the soup by placing a strainer over a large pot. Discard solids.

6. Consume immediately or transfer soup to a large glass container with a tight-fitting lid. Soup can be stored in the refrigerator for up to 5 days or in the freezer for up to 1 month.

Per serving:
Calories: 62
Fat: 1.8 grams
Protein: 4.2 grams

Sodium: 61 milligrams
Carbohydrates: 9.0 grams
Sugar: 3.1 grams
Fiber: 0.5 grams

Spicy Thai Chicken Broth

YIELDS 16 CUPS OR 8 SERVINGS

16 cups purified water

1 large chicken carcass

4 garlic cloves, chopped

4 cups chopped lemongrass

½ cup yellow miso paste

1. In a large pot, combine all ingredients, stirring to ensure miso paste is thoroughly combined.

2. Over high heat, bring soup to a boil, reduce heat to a simmer, and cover.

3. Allow soup to simmer for 4–24 hours.

4. Remove from heat and allow to cool.

5. Strain bones, lemongrass, and solids from the soup by placing a strainer over a large pot. Discard solids.

6. Consume immediately or transfer soup to a large glass container with a tight-fitting lid. Soup can be stored in the refrigerator for up to 5 days or in the freezer for up to 1 month.

Per serving:
Calories: 70
Fat: 2.8 grams
Protein: 5.4 grams
Sodium: 756 milligrams
Carbohydrates: 5.8 grams
Sugar: 1.2 grams
Fiber: 1.1 grams

Thanksgiving Turkey Broth

YIELDS 16 CUPS OR 8 SERVINGS

16 cups purified water

1 large turkey carcass

2 red onions, peeled and chopped

3 carrots, peeled and chopped

4 celery ribs, chopped

4 garlic cloves, chopped

1 cup crushed caraway seeds

½ cup chopped dried sage

3 cups chopped dried basil

1. In a large pot, combine all ingredients.
2. Over high heat, bring soup to a boil, reduce heat to a simmer, and cover.
3. Allow soup to simmer for 4–24 hours.
4. Remove from heat and allow to cool.
5. Strain bones, vegetables, and solids from the soup by placing a strainer over a large pot. Discard solids.
6. Consume immediately or transfer soup to a large glass container with a tight-fitting lid. Soup can be stored in the refrigerator for up to 5 days or in the freezer for up to 1 month.

Per serving:

Calories: 52

Fat: 1.7 grams

Protein: 4.6 grams

Sodium: 60 milligrams

Carbohydrates: 4.5 grams

Sugar: 1.2 grams

Fiber: 2.2 grams

Tomato-Basil Chicken Broth

YIELDS 16 CUPS OR 8 SERVINGS

16 cups purified water

1 large chicken carcass

4 garlic cloves, chopped

4 cups puréed tomatoes

3 cups chopped dried basil

1. In a large pot, combine all ingredients.
2. Over high heat, bring soup to a boil, reduce heat to a simmer, and cover.
3. Allow soup to simmer for 4–24 hours.
4. Remove from heat and allow to cool.
5. Strain bones, vegetables, and solids from the soup by placing a strainer over a large pot. Discard solids.
6. Consume immediately or transfer soup to a large glass container with a tight-fitting lid. Soup can be stored in the refrigerator for up to 5 days or in the freezer for up to 1 month.

Per serving:

Calories: 53

Fat: 2.1 grams

Protein: 4.0 grams

Sodium: 62 milligrams

Carbohydrates: 4.4 grams

Sugar: 1.7 grams

Fiber: 0.9 grams

Roasted Red Vegetable Broth

YIELDS 16 CUPS OR 8 SERVINGS

½ cup olive oil, divided

1 large chicken carcass

4 garlic cloves, chopped

2 large red onions, peeled and chopped

3 red bell peppers, peeled, seeded, and chopped

6 Roma tomatoes, sliced

3 cups chopped dried basil

16 cups purified water

1. Preheat oven to 400°F.

2. Evenly coat a roasting pan or baking sheet with ¼ cup olive oil. Place the carcass, garlic, onions, peppers, and tomatoes in the pan and drizzle ¼ cup olive oil over the chicken and vegetables; top with the basil.

3. Roast for 40 minutes, turning vegetables after 20 minutes.

4. Transfer all ingredients, with browned bits and oil, to a large pot. Cover with water. Over high heat, bring soup to a boil, reduce heat to a simmer, and cover.

5. Allow soup to simmer for 4–24 hours.

6. Remove from heat and allow to cool.

7. Strain bones, vegetables, and solids from the soup by placing a strainer over a large pot. Discard solids.

8. Consume immediately or transfer soup to a large glass container with a tight-fitting lid. Soup can be stored in the refrigerator for up to 5 days or in the freezer for up to 1 month.

Per serving:
Calories: 74
Fat: 4.9 grams
Protein: 3.6 grams

Sodium: 55 milligrams
Carbohydrates: 3.9 grams
Sugar: 2.1 grams
Fiber: 1.3 grams

Simple Vegetable-Based Poultry Broth

YIELDS 16 CUPS OR 8 SERVINGS

16 cups purified water

1 large chicken carcass

4 garlic cloves, chopped

4 cups freshly squeezed lemon juice

3 large carrots, peeled and chopped

4 celery ribs, chopped

2 zucchini, sliced

2 cups fresh green peas (may also be frozen and thawed)

2 cups fresh corn kernels (may also be frozen and thawed)

1. In a large pot, combine all ingredients.

2. Over high heat, bring soup to a boil, reduce heat to a simmer, and cover.

3. Allow soup to simmer for 4–24 hours.

4. Remove from heat and allow to cool.

5. Strain bones, vegetables, and solids from the soup by placing a strainer over a large pot. Discard solids.

6. Consume immediately or transfer soup to a large glass container with a tight-fitting lid. Soup can be stored in the refrigerator for up to 5 days or in the freezer for up to 1 month.

Per serving:
Calories: 72
Fat: 1.8 grams
Protein: 4.1 grams

Sodium: 72 milligrams
Carbohydrates: 9.8 grams
Sugar: 3.4 grams
Fiber: 0.6 grams

Tomato-Based Bone Broth

2 pounds beef bones

½ cup extra-virgin olive oil, divided

8 cups purified water

4 garlic cloves, chopped

8 cups tomato purée

3 cups chopped dried basil

1. Preheat oven to 400°F.

2. Evenly coat a large roasting pan or baking sheet with ¼ cup olive oil. Place the bones on the pan and drizzle with the remaining ¼ cup olive oil. Roast for 45 minutes, turning once after 20–25 minutes.

3. Pour bones and drippings into a large pot and add water, garlic, tomato, and basil.

4. Over high heat, bring soup to a boil, reduce heat to a simmer, and cover.

5. Allow soup to simmer for 4–24 hours.

6. Remove from heat and allow to cool.

7. Strain bones, vegetables, and solids from the soup by placing a strainer over a large pot. Discard solids.

8. Consume immediately or transfer soup to a large glass container with a tight-fitting lid. Soup can be stored in the refrigerator for up to 5 days or in the freezer for up to 1 month.

Per serving:
Calories: 106
Fat: 6.7 grams
Protein: 4.3 grams

Sodium: 52 milligrams
Carbohydrates: 7.2 grams
Sugar: 3.5 grams
Fiber: 1.6 grams

CHAPTER 11

Cold Soups

Sometimes it takes a cold soup to calm a craving. Whether you're trying to beat the heat of the summer sun or just have a craving for a refreshing bowl of chilled delicious-ness, this chapter of delightful cold soup recipes will fit your needs just perfectly. Here you'll find a variety of delicious and nutritious cold soup recipes—like Nutty Fruity Fig, Mediterranean Gazpacho with Rice Noodles, and Mango Cream with Ginger—that satisfy your taste buds and help you increase your energy levels, maximize your metabolic functioning, and satisfy the systems in your body that are responsible for everything from breathing to the beating of your heart. By consuming cold soups, you force your body's systems to work harder in order to regulate your body's temperature response to consuming cold fluids.

Sweet or savory, these cold soups pack tons of delightful ingredients like cucumbers, tomatoes, berries, tropical fruits, and citrus, and combine them with creamy additions or simple bone broths to make your lunch, dinner, or snack soup a cold combination of healthy ingredients that maximize flavor and nutrition. Improving your health has never tasted better than when fresh ingredients combine in your favorite delicious and nutritious recipes, and with vitamins, minerals, and potent phytochemicals filling every single sip of these cold soups, you can relax knowing that these delicious dishes are working hard to improve your health, happiness, and quality of life . . . and they taste great doing it!

Berry Banana Gazpacho

YIELDS 4 SERVINGS

8 cups vanilla almond milk

4 cups strawberries, tops removed

1 cup blueberries

2 bananas, peeled and halved

½ cup ground flaxseed

1. In a countertop blender, combine all ingredients.

2. Blend on high until all ingredients are broken down and thoroughly combined, about 2–3 minutes.

3. Consume immediately or transfer soup to a large glass container with a tight-fitting lid and store in the refrigerator for up to 5 days.

FROZEN BANANAS FOR AN EVEN SWEETER TREAT

When you peel and freeze bananas, you may be surprised to find your next frozen banana treat to be a little sweeter than you expected. If you wait until bananas are slightly overly ripened (when the exterior becomes dark brown) to peel and freeze them, you'll find that the resulting taste of any frozen, blended, or stewed treat you add them to has a slightly sweeter taste than if you had used fresh frozen bananas. So the next time you need a little extra sweetness and don't want to use sugar, use a frozen ripe banana instead.

Per serving:
Calories: 373
Fat: 11.5 grams
Protein: 5.9 grams

Sodium: 326 milligrams
Carbohydrates: 65.9 grams
Sugar: 49.9 grams
Fiber: 9.3 grams

Lemon-Asparagus Cream

YIELDS 4 SERVINGS

6 cups unsweetened almond milk

6 cups asparagus spears

1 cup lemon juice

2 cups Greek yogurt

1. In a large pot, combine almond milk, asparagus spears, and lemon.

2. Over high heat, bring to a boil, then reduce heat and simmer for 20 minutes or until asparagus is fork-tender.

3. Remove from heat and allow to cool for 2 hours.

4. Add Greek yogurt. Using an immersion blender, submerge blades and blend on high until asparagus is broken down and a creamy texture is achieved, about 5 minutes.

5. Consume immediately or transfer soup to a large glass container with a tight-fitting lid and store in the refrigerator for up to 5 days.

Per serving:
Calories: 193
Fat: 9.0 grams
Protein: 15.1 grams

Sodium: 279 milligrams
Carbohydrates: 16.0 grams
Sugar: 9.3 grams
Fiber: 4.4 grams

Nutty Fruity Fig

YIELDS 4 SERVINGS

8 cups vanilla almond milk

2 cups shelled walnuts

6 figs, stems removed

1 cup blueberries

1 cup chia seeds

1. In a countertop blender, combine all ingredients.

2. Blend on high until all ingredients are broken down and thoroughly combined, about 2–3 minutes.

3. Transfer soup to a large glass container with a tight-fitting lid and store in the refrigerator for 12–24 hours when a thicker consistency will develop. Soup can be stored in the refrigerator for up to 3 days.

Per serving:
Calories: 719
Fat: 44.4 grams
Protein: 14.6 grams

Sodium: 322 milligrams
Carbohydrates: 70.6 grams
Sugar: 52.6 grams
Fiber: 15.0 grams

Avocado-Cucumber-Melon

YIELDS 4 SERVINGS

6 cups unsweetened almond milk

2 Hass avocados, peeled and seeded

2 large cucumbers, peeled and halved

2 cups chopped honeydew melon

1. In a countertop blender, combine all ingredients.

2. Blend on high until all ingredients are broken down and thoroughly combined, about 2–3 minutes.

3. Consume immediately or transfer soup to a large glass container with a tight-fitting lid and store in the refrigerator for up to 5 days.

Per serving:
Calories: 217
Fat: 14.1 grams
Protein: 4.3 grams

Sodium: 264 milligrams
Carbohydrates: 17.2 grams
Sugar: 9.1 grams
Fiber: 6.8 grams

Green Gazpacho

YIELDS 4 SERVINGS

6 cups purified water

2 cups Greek yogurt

2 large cucumbers, peeled and chopped

6 tomatillos, chopped

2 large leeks, chopped

1 jalapeño pepper, ribs and seeds removed and minced

2 garlic cloves, minced

1. In a countertop blender, combine all ingredients.

2. Blend on high until all ingredients are broken down and thoroughly combined, about 2–3 minutes.

3. Consume immediately or transfer soup to a large glass container with a tight-fitting lid and store in the refrigerator for up to 5 days.

Per serving:
Calories: 158
Fat: 49 grams
Protein: 11.1 grams

Sodium: 61 milligrams
Carbohydrates: 17.0 grams
Sugar: 9.8 grams
Fiber: 2.9 grams

Mediterranean Gazpacho with Rice Noodles

YIELDS 4 SERVINGS

4 cups purified water

4 cups puréed tomatoes

1 cup quartered artichokes, crushed

1 cup chopped fresh basil

2 cups chopped spinach

1 tablespoon dried rosemary

1 tablespoon ground cumin

1 tablespoon ground coriander

1 tablespoon ground oregano

1 (16-ounce) package rice noodles, cooked

1. In a countertop blender, combine all ingredients except rice noodles.

2. Blend on high until all ingredients are broken down and thoroughly combined, about 2–3 minutes.

3. Transfer soup to a large bowl or glass container and stir in rice noodles until all ingredients are thoroughly combined.

4. Consume immediately or transfer soup to a large glass container with a tight-fitting lid and store in the refrigerator for up to 5 days.

Per serving:
Calories: 542
Fat: 2.4
Protein: 12.8 grams

Sodium: 165 milligrams
Carbohydrates: 121.7 grams
Sugar: 12.7 grams
Fiber: 10.6 grams

Sweet Southern Bisque with Corn, Vidalia, and Potato

YIELDS 4 SERVINGS

8 cups purified water

4 cups fresh corn kernels (may also use frozen and thawed)

2 large baking potatoes, cubed

2 cups chopped Vidalia onions

1. In a large pot over high heat, combine all ingredients.

2. Bring soup to a boil and reduce heat to a simmer.

3. Simmer for 30–40 minutes or until potatoes are fork-tender.

4. Using an immersion blender, submerge blades in soup and blend on high until all ingredients are broken down and thoroughly combined and desired consistency is achieved, about 5 minutes.

5. Allow soup to cool completely and refrigerate for 6–8 hours before serving.

6. Transfer remaining soup to a large glass container with a tight-fitting lid and store in the refrigerator for up to 5 days.

THE IMPORTANCE OF ORGANICS

With increasing scientific evidence showing the devastating health effects of pesticides, herbicides, and toxins used in the production of produce, it is absolutely imperative to choose organic produce. Nonorganic corn, especially, has been shown to have negative effects on digestion, cognition, respiratory health, and much more. With soups that are designed for your soup cleanse routine, it's highly recommended that you opt for produce that is organic and at its freshest point, ensuring that the taste of your delicious and nutritious soups is exactly as it is intended. When you're dealing with a perfect cold soup ingredient like corn, which can be enjoyed both hot or cold, it's imperative that you purchase organic.

Per serving:
Calories: 304
Fat: 1.1 grams
Protein: 8.8 grams

Sodium: 35 milligrams
Carbohydrates: 71.2 grams
Sugar: 10.2 grams
Fiber: 7.1 grams

Minty Cucumber

YIELDS 4 SERVINGS

4 cups vanilla almond milk

2 cups Greek yogurt

2 cups vanilla kefir

3 large cucumbers, peeled with ends removed

2 cups chopped fresh mint leaves

1. In a countertop blender, combine all ingredients.

2. Blend on high until all ingredients are broken down and thoroughly combined, about 2–3 minutes.

3. Consume immediately or transfer soup to a large glass container with a tight-fitting lid and store in the refrigerator for up to 5 days.

Per serving:
Calories: 298
Fat: 9.6 grams
Protein: 15.7 grams

Sodium: 245 milligrams
Carbohydrates: 39.4 grams
Sugar: 34.4 grams
Fiber: 3.5 grams

Red Fruit Roundup

YIELDS 4 SERVINGS

6 cups vanilla almond milk

2 cups vanilla kefir

1 cup strawberries, tops removed

1 cup raspberries

2 cups pomegranate jewels

1. In a countertop blender, combine all ingredients.

2. Blend on high until all ingredients are broken down and thoroughly combined, about 2–3 minutes.

3. Consume immediately or transfer soup to a large glass container with a tight-fitting lid and store in the refrigerator for up to 5 days.

Per serving:
Calories: 314
Fat: 7.0 grams
Protein: 7.5 grams

Sodium: 286 milligrams
Carbohydrates: 59.4 grams
Sugar: 50.6 grams
Fiber: 7.2 grams

Spicy Jalapeño Cucumber

YIELDS 4 SERVINGS

6 cups almond milk

2 cups Greek yogurt

3 jalapeño peppers, ribs and seeds removed

3 large cucumbers, peeled with ends removed

1. In a countertop blender, combine all ingredients.

2. Blend on high until all ingredients are broken down and thoroughly combined, about 2–3 minutes.

3. Consume immediately or transfer soup to a large glass container with a tight-fitting lid and store in the refrigerator for up to 5 days.

CAPSAICIN FOR IMPROVED OVERALL HEALTH

The spicy kick you get from the delicious addition of peppers like jalapeños is all thanks to a naturally occurring phytochemical, capsaicin. Not only does this potent phytochemical add tons of fiery flavor to your favorite recipes, but it actually contributes to the body's overall health. From cleansing the blood to improving digestion, boosting metabolism, and sharpening mental focus, this delicious ingredient adds a heaping helping of health-boosting qualities as well as heat!

Per serving:
Calories: 213
Fat: 8.8 grams
Protein: 11.8 grams

Sodium: 279 milligrams
Carbohydrates: 21.2 grams
Sugar: 17.8 grams
Fiber: 1.8 grams

Garlicky Sweet Pea

YIELDS 4 SERVINGS

6 cups almond milk

2 cups Greek yogurt

4 cloves garlic, peeled

4 cups sweet peas

1 tablespoon garlic powder

1. In a countertop blender, combine all ingredients.

2. Blend on high until all ingredients are broken down and thoroughly combined, about 2–3 minutes.

3. Consume immediately or transfer soup to a large glass container with a tight-fitting lid and store in the refrigerator for up to 5 days.

Per serving:
Calories: 314
Fat: 9.2 grams
Protein: 19.0 grams

Sodium: 284 milligrams
Carbohydrates: 39.7 grams
Sugar: 22.8 grams
Fiber: 7.7 grams

Cubanelle Cucumber with Garlic

YIELDS 4 SERVINGS

6 cups almond milk

2 cups Greek yogurt

3 cubanelle peppers, ribs and seeds removed

3 large cucumbers, peeled with ends removed

3 garlic cloves, peeled

1. In a countertop blender, combine all ingredients.

2. Blend on high until all ingredients are broken down and thoroughly combined, about 2–3 minutes.

3. Consume immediately or transfer soup to a large glass container with a tight-fitting lid and store in the refrigerator for up to 5 days.

Per serving:
Calories: 226
Fat: 8.8 grams
Protein: 12.6 grams

Sodium: 282 milligrams
Carbohydrates: 24.3 grams
Sugar: 18.9 grams
Fiber: 2.3 grams

Cool Classic Tomato

YIELDS 4 SERVINGS

4 cups Greek yogurt

4 cups puréed tomatoes

8 large Roma tomatoes, chopped

2 garlic cloves, peeled

2 tablespoons garlic powder

2 tablespoons ground black pepper

1. In a countertop blender, combine all ingredients.

2. Blend on high until all ingredients are broken down and thoroughly combined, about 2–3 minutes.

3. Consume immediately or transfer soup to a large glass container with a tight-fitting lid and store in the refrigerator for up to 5 days.

Per serving:
Calories: 365
Fat: 12.4 grams
Protein: 24.6 grams

Sodium: 150 milligrams
Carbohydrates: 47.2 grams
Sugar: 32.1 grams
Fiber: 7.7 grams

Cool Zucchini Soup

YIELDS 4 SERVINGS

4 cups almond milk

2 cups Greek yogurt

2 cups vanilla kefir

3 zucchini, ends removed

1 cup chopped fresh mint leaves

1. In a countertop blender, combine all ingredients.

2. Blend on high until all ingredients are broken down and thoroughly combined, about 2–3 minutes.

3. Consume immediately or transfer soup to a large glass container with a tight-fitting lid and store in the refrigerator for up to 5 days.

Per serving:
Calories: 264
Fat: 10.0 grams
Protein: 16.0 grams

Sodium: 251 milligrams
Carbohydrates: 30.5 grams
Sugar: 26.2 grams
Fiber: 3.0 grams

White Bean and Vegetable

YIELDS 4 SERVINGS

4 cups purified water

4 cups tomato purée

3 cups canned great northern beans (may also use dried beans that have been soaked for 24 hours)

2 carrots, peeled and chopped

2 celery ribs, chopped

2 cups Vidalia onions, chopped

2 garlic cloves, minced

1. Combine all ingredients in a large pot.

2. Over high heat, bring soup to a boil and reduce to a simmer.

3. Simmer for 30 minutes or until beans and vegetables are tender.

4. Remove from heat and allow to cool. Transfer soup to a large glass container with a tight-fitting lid and refrigerate for 6–8 hours before serving.

5. Consume immediately and store remaining soup in a large glass container with a tight-fitting lid in the refrigerator for up to 5 days or in the freezer for up to 14 days.

Per serving:
Calories: 258
Fat: 0.4 grams
Protein: 14.3 grams

Sodium: 467 milligrams
Carbohydrates: 58.0 grams
Sugar: 17.8 grams
Fiber: 15.7 grams

Cool Minestrone

4 cups purified water

4 cups tomato purée

1 cup canned kidney beans (may also use dried beans that have been soaked for 24 hours)

1 cup canned great northern beans (may also use dried beans that have been soaked for 24 hours)

1 cup canned black beans (may also use dried beans that have been soaked for 24 hours)

1 large Idaho potato, cubed into ¼" pieces

2 celery stalks, chopped

2 carrots, peeled and chopped

1 cup chopped green cabbage

4 garlic cloves, minced

1. Combine all ingredients in a large pot.

2. Over high heat, bring soup to a boil and reduce to a simmer.

3. Simmer for 30 minutes or until beans and vegetables are tender.

4. Remove from heat and allow to cool. Transfer soup to a large glass container with a tight-fitting lid and refrigerate for 6–8 hours before serving.

5. Consume immediately and store remaining soup in an airtight container in the refrigerator for up to 5 days.

Per serving:
Calories: 341
Fat: 1.1 grams
Protein: 17.6 grams

Sodium: 508 milligrams
Carbohydrates: 72.2 grams
Sugar: 17.3 grams
Fiber: 17.8 grams

Sweet Beet Treat

YIELDS 4 SERVINGS

4 tablespoons coconut oil, divided

4 red beets, greens removed

4 golden beets, greens removed

4 cups vanilla almond milk

2 cups Greek yogurt

2 cups vanilla kefir

1. Preheat oven to 400°F.

2. Evenly coat a large baking sheet or roasting pan with 2 tablespoons coconut oil. Rinse beets, cut into halves, and place on prepared baking sheet. Drizzle with the remaining 2 tablespoons coconut oil.

3. Roast for 1 hour, turning after 30 minutes.

4. Remove from heat and allow to cool for 1 hour.

5. In a countertop blender, combine all ingredients.

6. Blend on high until all ingredients are broken down and thoroughly combined, about 3–5 minutes.

7. Consume immediately or transfer soup to a large glass container with a tight-fitting lid and store in the refrigerator for up to 5 days.

Per serving:

Calories: 395

Fat: 18.0 grams

Protein: 16.6 grams

Sodium: 385 milligrams

Carbohydrates: 41.2 grams

Sugar: 37.1 grams

Fiber: 6.1 grams

Mango Cream with Ginger

YIELDS 4 SERVINGS

6 cups almond milk

3" piece of ginger, peeled

4 mangoes, peeled and seeded

2 cups vanilla kefir

1. In a countertop blender, combine almond milk and ginger and blend on high until ginger is completely broken down, about 2–3 minutes.

2. Add mangoes and kefir and blend on high until all ingredients are broken down and thoroughly combined, about 2–3 minutes.

3. Consume immediately or transfer soup to a large glass container with a tight-fitting lid and store in the refrigerator for up to 5 days.

Per serving:	
Calories: 295	Sodium: 284 milligrams
Fat: 6.6 grams	Carbohydrates: 56.1 grams
Protein: 7.3 grams	Sugar: 30.7 grams
	Fiber: 4.1 grams

Fruity Avocado Cucumber

YIELDS 4 SERVINGS

8 cups coconut milk

1 cup strawberries, tops removed

2 kiwis, peeled

2 Hass avocados, peeled and seeded

1 large cucumber, peeled with ends removed

¼ cup ground flaxseed

1. In a countertop blender, combine all ingredients.

2. Blend on high until all ingredients are broken down and thoroughly combined, about 2–3 minutes.

3. Consume immediately or transfer soup to a large glass container with a tight-fitting lid and store in the refrigerator for up to 5 days.

Per serving:	
Calories: 363	Sodium: 80 milligrams
Fat: 23.5 grams	Carbohydrates: 31.8 grams
Protein: 3.5 grams	Sugar: 20.1 grams
	Fiber: 9.4 grams

Spiced Acorn Squash

YIELDS 4 SERVINGS

4 tablespoons coconut oil, divided

2 acorn squash, halved and seeded

2 tablespoons ground cinnamon

2 tablespoons ground cardamom

2 tablespoons dried rosemary

8 cups vanilla almond milk

1. Preheat oven to 400°F.

2. Evenly coat a large baking sheet or roasting pan with 2 tablespoons coconut oil. Place squash inner-side up on prepared pan. Drizzle with the remaining 2 tablespoons coconut oil.

3. Roast for 1 hour, turning after 30 minutes.

4. Allow to cool for 1 hour. Scoop the flesh away from the skin and discard the skin.

5. In a countertop blender, combine all ingredients.

6. Blend on high until all ingredients are thoroughly combined, about 2–3 minutes. Consume immediately or transfer soup to a large glass container with a tight-fitting lid and store in the refrigerator for up to 5 days.

Per serving:

Calories: 348

Fat: 11.9 grams

Protein: 4.3 grams

Sodium: 328 milligrams

Carbohydrates: 60.7 grams

Sugar: 32.1 grams

Fiber: 6.6 grams

Creamy Tomato Basil

YIELDS 4 SERVINGS

2 cups almond milk

4 cups tomato purée

2 cups Greek yogurt

6 large Roma tomatoes

2 cups chopped fresh basil

1. In a countertop blender, combine all ingredients.

2. Blend on high until all ingredients are broken down and thoroughly combined.

3. Consume immediately or transfer soup to a large glass container with a tight-fitting lid and store in the refrigerator for up to 5 days.

Per serving:
Calories: 275
Fat: 8.1 grams
Protein: 15.5 grams

Sodium: 192 milligrams
Carbohydrates: 41.3 grams
Sugar: 28.6 grams
Fiber: 6.4 grams

Pear-Apple-Cucumber Cream

YIELDS 4 SERVINGS

6 cups vanilla almond milk

2 cups vanilla kefir

2 Bartlett pears, peeled and cored

2 Fuji apples, peeled and cored

2 cucumbers, peeled with ends removed

1. In a countertop blender, combine all ingredients.

2. Blend on high until all ingredients are broken down and thoroughly combined, about 2–3 minutes.

3. Consume immediately or transfer soup to a large glass container with a tight-fitting lid and store in the refrigerator for up to 5 days.

Per serving:
Calories: 326
Fat: 5.8 grams
Protein: 6.9 grams

Sodium: 286 milligrams
Carbohydrates: 63.6 grams
Sugar: 54.1 grams
Fiber: 5.8 grams

CHAPTER 12

Dessert Soups

Sometimes, the craving for something sweet just can't be calmed without satisfying the sweet tooth, but the urge to calm cravings for sweetness with processed foods packed with sugar, fat, and preservatives can quickly unravel all of your efforts to soup cleanse for health benefits of all kinds. In this chapter, you'll find healthy soups like Cinnamon Cream Dream, Peach Cobbler, Nutty Oats and Honey, and Cucumber-Kiwi Coconut Cream that are packed with a delightful combination of whole foods like fruits and vegetables and healthy additions like flaxseed and chia seeds that can help you meet your sweet needs, but won't sabotage your soup-cleansing goals. With perfect produce combinations like berries, citrus, pears, peaches, mangoes, pineapple, and grapes, combined with light-tasting vegetables or sweet vegetables, and creamy additions like nut milks, coconut milk, yogurt, and kefir, these delicious recipes help you keep your health goals on track with vitamins, minerals, and probiotic-rich ingredients that will help you naturally boost your immunity, improve skin conditions, and optimize your overall health. Now you can have dessert and sip it, too!

Sweet Potato Pie

YIELDS 4 SERVINGS

6 cups purified water, plus more as needed

2 large sweet potatoes, scrubbed and chopped

2 tablespoons coconut oil

2 teaspoons ground cinnamon

2 teaspoons ground cardamom

2 teaspoons ground cloves

4 cups unsweetened vanilla almond milk

1. Combine water and sweet potatoes in a large pot, adding additional water (if needed) to cover potatoes.

2. Bring potatoes to a boil, reduce heat to a simmer, and cover. Simmer for 20–25 minutes or until fork-tender.

3. Remove from heat. Add coconut oil, cinnamon, cardamom, cloves, and almond milk.

4. Using an immersion blender, submerge blades and blend until all sweet potatoes are smooth and desired consistency is achieved, about 5 minutes.

5. Consume immediately or transfer soup to a large glass container with a tight-fitting lid and store in the refrigerator for up to 3–5 days.

Per serving:
Calories: 153
Fat: 9.0 grams
Protein: 2.2 grams

Sodium: 212 milligrams
Carbohydrates: 15.5 grams
Sugar: 2.8 grams
Fiber: 3.3 grams

Blueberry Muffin

YIELDS 4 SERVINGS

4 cups blueberries

1 cup uncooked rolled oats

2 teaspoons ground cinnamon

6 cups unsweetened vanilla almond milk

1. Combine all ingredients in a countertop blender.

2. Blend on high until all ingredients are broken down and thoroughly combined, about 2–3 minutes.

3. Consume immediately or transfer soup to a large glass container with a tight-fitting lid and store in the refrigerator for up to 3–5 days.

Per serving:
Calories: 207
Fat: 5.6 grams
Protein: 5.2 grams

Sodium: 241 milligrams
Carbohydrates: 36.0 grams
Sugar: 15.3 grams
Fiber: 6.2 grams

Cinnamon Cream Dream

YIELDS 4 SERVINGS

4 cups vanilla almond milk

2 cups Greek yogurt

2 cups kefir

4 tablespoons ground cinnamon

2 teaspoons ground cardamom

1. Combine all ingredients in a countertop blender.

2. Blend on high until all ingredients are broken down and thoroughly combined, about 2–3 minutes.

3. Consume immediately or transfer soup to a large glass container with a tight-fitting lid and store in the refrigerator for up to 3–5 days.

Per serving:
Calories: 288
Fat: 11.6 grams
Protein: 14.4 grams

Sodium: 258 milligrams
Carbohydrates: 34.5 grams
Sugar: 26.2 grams
Fiber: 5.9 grams

Apple Pie à la Mode

YIELDS 4 SERVINGS
6 cups vanilla almond milk

2 cups vanilla kefir

½ cup uncooked rolled oats

6 Fuji apples, peeled and cored

2 teaspoons ground cinnamon

2 teaspoons ground cloves

1. Combine all ingredients in a countertop blender.

2. Blend on high until all ingredients are broken down and thoroughly combined, about 2–3 minutes.

3. Consume immediately or transfer soup to a large glass container with a tight-fitting lid and store in the refrigerator for up to 3–5 days.

Per serving:
Calories: 374
Fat: 6.7 grams
Protein: 7.5 grams

Sodium: 285 milligrams
Carbohydrates: 76.3 grams
Sugar: 60.2 grams
Fiber: 6.2 grams

Piña Colada

YIELDS 4 SERVINGS
4 cups coconut milk

2 cups vanilla kefir

4 cups chopped pineapple

1 cup unsweetened coconut flakes

1. Combine all ingredients in a countertop blender.

2. Blend on high until all ingredients are broken down and thoroughly combined, about 2–3 minutes.

3. Consume immediately or transfer soup to a large glass container with a tight-fitting lid and store in the refrigerator for up to 3–5 days.

Per serving:
Calories: 292
Fat: 12.1 grams
Protein: 5.4 grams

Sodium: 81 milligrams
Carbohydrates: 43.7 grams
Sugar: 35.3 grams
Fiber: 4.3 grams

Watermelon-Mint

YIELDS 4 SERVINGS

4 cups purified water

6 cups chopped watermelon

1 cup chopped fresh mint leaves

1. Combine all ingredients in a countertop blender.

2. Blend on high until all ingredients are broken down and thoroughly combined, about 2–3 minutes.

3. Consume immediately or transfer soup to a large glass container with a tight-fitting lid and store in the refrigerator for up to 3–5 days.

Per serving:
Calories: 72
Fat: 0.3 grams
Protein: 1.6 grams

Sodium: 13 milligrams
Carbohydrates: 18.2 grams
Sugar: 14.1 grams
Fiber: 1.4 grams

Cinnamon-Almond Dessert Soup

YIELDS 4 SERVINGS

8 cups vanilla almond milk

4 cups raw almonds

2 tablespoons coconut oil

2 teaspoons ground cinnamon

2 teaspoons ground cardamom

2 teaspoons ground cloves

1. Combine all ingredients in a countertop blender and blend on high until almonds are broken down and all ingredients are thoroughly combined, about 2–3 minutes.

2. Consume immediately or transfer soup to a large glass container with a tight-fitting lid and store in the refrigerator for up to 3–5 days.

Per serving:
Calories: 1072
Fat: 83.9 grams
Protein: 32.6 grams

Sodium: 323 milligrams
Carbohydrates: 62.6 grams
Sugar: 39.0 grams
Fiber: 18.2 grams

Peach Cobbler

YIELDS 4 SERVINGS

6 cups vanilla almond milk
6 peaches, pitted and quartered
2 teaspoons ground cinnamon
2 teaspoons ground cloves
½ cup ground flaxseed
2 cups honey kefir

1. Combine almond milk, peaches, cinnamon, and cloves in a large pot.

2. Bring soup to a boil, reduce heat to a simmer, and cover.

3. Simmer for 20 minutes or until peaches are fork-tender.

4. Remove from heat, add flaxseed, and stir to combine.

5. Allow to cool for 1 hour.

6. Add kefir. Using an immersion blender, submerge blades and blend until peaches are broken down and all ingredients are thoroughly combined, about 5 minutes.

7. Consume immediately or transfer soup to a large glass container with a tight-fitting lid and store in the refrigerator for up to 3–5 days.

BETA CAROTENE–RICH PEACHES

Beta carotene is a phytochemical that is essential for optimal health. Also known as vitamin A, beta carotene gives orange and yellow fruits and vegetables their vibrant hue and helps preserve the health of the eyes, heart, and bones. Beta carotene–rich foods like the peaches included in this delightful dessert recipe are absolutely a delicious and nutritious addition to any soup cleanse routine geared toward great health!

Per serving:
Calories: 412
Fat: 11.4 grams
Protein: 11.7 grams

Sodium: 331 milligrams
Carbohydrates: 70.2 grams
Sugar: 61.9 grams
Fiber: 8.4 grams

Sweet Spiced Cherries and Cream

YIELDS 4 SERVINGS

6 cups vanilla almond milk

6 cups pitted cherries

1" piece of ginger, peeled and grated

2 teaspoons ground cinnamon

2 teaspoons ground cardamom

2 teaspoons ground cloves

1 cup Greek yogurt

1 cup vanilla kefir

1. Combine almond milk, cherries, ginger, cinnamon, cardamom, and cloves in a large pot.

2. Bring to a boil, reduce heat to a simmer, and cover.

3. Simmer for 20 minutes or until cherries are fork-tender.

4. Remove from heat and allow to cool for 1 hour.

5. Add Greek yogurt and kefir. Using an immersion blender, submerge blades and blend until all ingredients are broken down and thoroughly combined, about 5 minutes.

6. Consume immediately or transfer soup to a large glass container with a tight-fitting lid and store in the refrigerator for up to 3–5 days.

Per serving:

Calories: 377

Fat: 7.7 grams

Protein: 10.7 grams

Sodium: 281 milligrams

Carbohydrates: 72.0 grams

Sugar: 61.4 grams

Fiber: 6.7 grams

Mock Chocolate and Almond Butter Cream

YIELDS 4 SERVINGS

6 cups vanilla almond milk

2 cups raw almonds

6 figs, stems removed and halved

2 teaspoons ground cinnamon

2 cups vanilla kefir

1. Combine almond milk and almonds in a countertop blender and blend on high until almonds are broken down and thoroughly combined, about 2–3 minutes.

2. Add figs, cinnamon, and kefir to the blender and blend on high until figs are broken down and all ingredients are well blended, about 2–3 minutes.

3. Consume immediately or transfer soup to a large glass container with a tight-fitting lid and store in the refrigerator for up to 3–5 days.

BEWARE OF SNEAKY SUGARS

Sweet treats like confectionary creations and decadent desserts are well-known sugar-laden foods, but many other sources of sugar can be less obvious and sometimes surprising. If you choose to indulge in sweet sips of chocolate milk, sweetened coffees, sweet teas, and sodas, you may be surprised at their sugar content. To avoid excessive sugar intake (and the unavoidable sugar crash that follows), whip up an all-natural sweet treat like these delicious dessert recipes that will keep your sweet tooth satisfied and your soup cleanse on track for success!

Per serving:
Calories: 701
Fat: 42.2 grams
Protein: 21.5 grams

Sodium: 283 milligrams
Carbohydrates: 70.6 grams
Sugar: 54.6 grams
Fiber: 12.9 grams

Sweet and Spicy Quinoa with Figs

YIELDS 4 SERVINGS

6 cups vanilla almond milk

2" piece of ginger, peeled and grated

5 figs, stems removed and halved

2 tablespoons ground cinnamon

1 tablespoon ground cardamom

1 tablespoon ground cloves

2 cups cooked quinoa

1. Combine almond milk, ginger, figs, cinnamon, cardamom, and cloves in a large pot.

2. Bring soup to a boil, reduce heat to a simmer, and cover.

3. Simmer for 20 minutes or until figs are fork-tender.

4. Remove from heat and cool for 5 minutes.

5. Using an immersion blender, submerge blades and blend until all ingredients are broken down and well combined, about 5 minutes.

6. Add quinoa and stir to combine thoroughly.

7. Consume immediately or transfer soup to a large glass container with a tight-fitting lid and store in the refrigerator for up to 3–5 days.

Per serving:
Calories: 324
Fat: 5.9 grams
Protein: 6.6 grams

Sodium: 252 milligrams
Carbohydrates: 64.4 grams
Sugar: 38.0 grams
Fiber: 8.0 grams

Nutty Oats and Honey

YIELDS 4 SERVINGS

8 cups vanilla almond milk

2 cups raw almonds

½ cup ground flaxseed

½ cup raw organic honey

2 cups cooked steel-ground oats

1. Combine almond milk and almonds in a countertop blender and blend on high until almonds are crushed and thoroughly combined, about 2–3 minutes.

2. Add flaxseed and honey and blend on high until all ingredients are well blended, about 1–2 minutes.

3. Transfer soup to a different container and stir in oats. Stir to combine thoroughly.

4. Consume immediately or transfer soup to a large glass container with a tight-fitting lid and store in the refrigerator for up to 3–5 days.

Per serving:
Calories: 827
Fat: 47.9
Protein: 20.5 grams

Sodium: 327 milligrams
Carbohydrates: 90.4 grams
Sugar: 70.4 grams
Fiber: 13.3 grams

Figgy Pudding

YIELDS 4 SERVINGS

8 cups vanilla almond milk

8 figs, ends removed and skins intact

2 tablespoons coconut oil

2 teaspoons ground cinnamon

2 teaspoons ground cardamom

2 teaspoons ground cloves

2 cups chia seeds

1. In a large glass container with a tight-fitting lid, combine all ingredients and stir to blend thoroughly.

2. Using an immersion blender, submerge blades and blend until figs are broken down and desired consistency is achieved, about 5 minutes.

3. Allow to set for 12–18 hours or until pudding-like consistency is achieved.

4. Consume immediately or store in the refrigerator for up to 3–5 days.

Per serving:
Calories: 621
Fat: 30.5 grams
Protein: 12.5 grams

Sodium: 324 milligrams
Carbohydrates: 77.6 grams
Sugar: 52.9 grams
Fiber: 23.7 grams

Spiced Nuts

YIELDS 4 SERVINGS

8 cups vanilla almond milk

2 cups raw almonds

2 cups raw cashews

2 cups shelled walnuts

2 teaspoons ground cinnamon

2 teaspoons ground cardamom

2 teaspoons ground cloves

½ cup ground flaxseed

1. Combine all ingredients except flaxseed in a large pot.

2. Over high heat, bring soup to a boil, reduce heat to a simmer, and cover.

3. Simmer for 20–25 minutes or until nuts are soft.

4. Remove from heat and add flaxseed.

5. Using an immersion blender, submerge blades and blend until all ingredients are broken down and a smooth consistency is achieved, about 5 minutes.

6. Consume immediately or transfer soup to a large glass container with a tight-fitting lid and store in the refrigerator for up to 3–5 days.

Per serving:
Calories: 1489
Fat: 120.3 grams
Protein: 43.1 grams

Sodium: 336 milligrams
Carbohydrates: 83.2 grams
Sugar: 42.0 grams
Fiber: 20.3 grams

Sweet Spiced Grains with Fruit

YIELDS 4 SERVINGS

8 cups vanilla almond milk

2 large sweet potatoes, cut into ¼" cubes

2 tablespoons coconut oil

2 teaspoons ground cinnamon

2 teaspoons ground cardamom

2 teaspoons ground cloves

1 cup strawberries, tops removed

1 cup blueberries

1 cup cooked long-grain brown rice

1. Combine almond milk, sweet potatoes, coconut oil, cinnamon, cardamom, and cloves in a large pot.

2. Bring soup to a boil, reduce heat to a simmer, and cover.

3. Simmer for 20–25 minutes or until sweet potatoes are fork-tender.

4. Remove from heat and allow to cool for 5 minutes.

5. Using an immersion blender, submerge blades and blend until all sweet potatoes are smooth and desired consistency is achieved, about 5 minutes.

6. Stir in berries and rice until combined thoroughly.

7. Consume immediately or transfer soup to a large glass container with a tight-fitting lid and store in the refrigerator for up to 3–5 days.

Per serving:
Calories: 389
Fat: 12.1 grams
Protein: 5.0 grams
Sodium: 361 milligrams
Carbohydrates: 66.8 grams
Sugar: 40.4 grams
Fiber: 5.8 grams

Fruity Parfait

YIELDS 4 SERVINGS

6 cups coconut milk

2 cups chopped pineapple

2 cups strawberries, tops removed

2 cups blueberries

2 cups vanilla kefir

1. Combine coconut milk and pineapple in a countertop blender and blend on high until pineapple is broken down and thoroughly combined with the coconut milk, about 2–3 minutes.

2. Transfer soup to a large dish with a tight-fitting lid, add berries and kefir, and stir well to combine thoroughly.

3. Consume immediately or store in the refrigerator for up to 3–5 days.

BROMELAIN FOR BRUISES

Pineapple is a delicious and nutritious addition to dessert recipes that adds a unique sweetness as well as provides a unique health benefit. A unique phytochemical in pineapples, bromelain, acts to cleanse the blood of damaged blood vessels that cause the appearance of a bruise through the skin's surface. Bromelain's purging of dead or damaged blood vessels can reduce the appearance of a bruise in a fraction of the time if not treated at all.

Per serving:

Calories: 306

Fat: 9.8 grams

Protein: 5.5 grams

Sodium: 96 milligrams

Carbohydrates: 50.6 grams

Sugar: 41.0 grams

Fiber: 5.4 grams

Almond Butter Banana

YIELDS 4 SERVINGS

6 cups vanilla almond milk

2 cups raw almonds

2 teaspoons ground cloves

4 large bananas, peeled and halved

1 tablespoon freshly squeezed lemon juice

1. Combine almond milk, almonds, and cloves in a countertop blender and blend on high until almonds are broken down and thoroughly combined, about 2–3 minutes.

2. Add bananas and lemon juice and blend on high until thoroughly combined, about 2–3 minutes.

3. Consume immediately or transfer soup to a large glass container with a tight-fitting lid and store in the refrigerator for up to 3–5 days.

Per serving:	
Calories: 672	Sodium: 244 milligrams
Fat: 40.3 grams	Carbohydrates: 70.1 grams
Protein: 18.3 grams	Sugar: 44.2 grams
	Fiber: 12.4 grams

Strawberry Shortcake

YIELDS 4 SERVINGS

8 cups vanilla almond milk

5 cups strawberries, tops removed and halved

1 tablespoon maple syrup

1 tablespoon freshly squeezed lemon juice

2 cups cooked steel-ground oats

1 tablespoon ground cinnamon

1. Combine all ingredients in a countertop blender and blend on high until broken down and thoroughly blended, about 2–3 minutes.

2. Consume immediately or transfer soup to a large glass container with a tight-fitting lid and store in the refrigerator for up to 3–5 days.

Per serving:	
Calories: 338	Sodium: 326 milligrams
Fat: 7.2 grams	Carbohydrates: 65.1 grams
Protein: 6.3 grams	Sugar: 44.3 grams
	Fiber: 6.7 grams

Sweet Green Yogurt Dessert

YIELDS 4 SERVINGS

6 cups vanilla almond milk

2 cups vanilla kefir

2" piece of ginger, peeled and grated

2 large Hass avocados, peeled and pitted

½ cup raw organic honey

2 tablespoons freshly squeezed lemon juice

1. Combine all ingredients in a blender.

2. Blend on high until all ingredients are broken down and thoroughly combined, about 2–3 minutes.

3. Consume immediately or transfer soup to a large glass container with a tight-fitting lid and store in the refrigerator for up to 3–5 days.

HONEY'S AMAZING HEALTH BENEFITS

While most people love honey because of its unique taste and sweetness, few are aware of the many health benefits of this delicious and nutritious product. Acting as an antiviral, antibacterial, and antimicrobial agent, honey can help improve the immune system and safeguard the body, its systems, and its cells from infiltration of germs, bacteria, and viruses. In addition, this sweet treat can be placed on the skin to relieve burns and stings and prevent infections of wounds.

Per serving:
Calories: 471
Fat: 16.1 grams
Protein: 7.1 grams

Sodium: 290 milligrams
Carbohydrates: 79.1 grams
Sugar: 70.1 grams
Fiber: 6.2 grams

Nut Butter and Jelly

YIELDS 4 SERVINGS

6 cups vanilla almond milk

2 cups raw almonds

2 cups organic apple juice (not from concentrate)

2 cups strawberries, tops removed

2 cups blueberries

1 banana, peeled and halved

1. Combine almond milk and almonds in a countertop blender and blend on high until nuts are broken down and fully blended, about 2–3 minutes.

2. Add apple juice, berries, and banana and blend on high until thoroughly combined, about 2–3 minutes.

3. Consume immediately or transfer soup to a large glass container with a tight-fitting lid and store in the refrigerator for up to 3–5 days.

Per serving:
Calories: 695
Fat: 40.4 grams
Protein: 18.2 grams

Sodium: 246 milligrams
Carbohydrates: 75.1 grams
Sugar: 53.9 grams
Fiber: 12.7 grams

Cucumber-Kiwi Coconut Cream

YIELDS 4 SERVINGS

4 cups coconut milk

2 cups vanilla kefir

4 kiwis, peeled

3 cucumbers, peeled with ends removed and halved

1. Combine coconut milk, kefir, kiwis, and cucumbers in a countertop blender.

2. Blend on high until ingredients are broken down and thoroughly combined, about 2–3 minutes.

3. Consume immediately or transfer soup to a large glass container with a tight-fitting lid and store in the refrigerator for 3–5 days.

Per serving:
Calories: 227
Fat: 7.3 grams
Protein: 6.0 grams

Sodium: 83 milligrams
Carbohydrates: 34.7 grams
Sugar: 27.6 grams
Fiber: 4.5 grams

CONVERSION CHARTS

VOLUME CONVERSIONS

U.S. Volume Measure	Metric Equivalent
⅛ teaspoon	0.5 milliliter
¼ teaspoon	1 milliliter
½ teaspoon	2 milliliters
1 teaspoon	5 milliliters
½ tablespoon	7 milliliters
1 tablespoon (3 teaspoons)	15 milliliters
2 tablespoons (1 fluid ounce)	30 milliliters
¼ cup (4 tablespoons)	60 milliliters
⅓ cup	90 milliliters
½ cup (4 fluid ounces)	125 milliliters
⅔ cup	160 milliliters
¾ cup (6 fluid ounces)	180 milliliters
1 cup (16 tablespoons)	250 milliliters
1 pint (2 cups)	500 milliliters
1 quart (4 cups)	1 liter (about)

WEIGHT CONVERSIONS

U.S. Weight Measure	Metric Equivalent
½ ounce	15 grams
1 ounce	30 grams
2 ounces	60 grams
3 ounces	85 grams
¼ pound (4 ounces)	115 grams
½ pound (8 ounces)	225 grams
¾ pound (12 ounces)	340 grams
1 pound (16 ounces)	454 grams

LENGTH CONVERSIONS

U.S. Length Measure	Metric Equivalent
¼ inch	0.6 centimeters
½ inch	1.2 centimeters
¾ inch	1.9 centimeters
1 inch	2.5 centimeters
1½ inches	3.8 centimeters
1 foot	0.3 meters
1 yard	0.9 meters

About the Author

Britt Brandon is a Certified Personal Trainer and Certified Fitness Nutrition Specialist (certified by the International Sports Science Association, ISSA) who has enjoyed writing books focusing on clean eating and fitness for Adams Media for the past five years. She is the author of many books, including *Apple Cider Vinegar for Health*, *Coconut Oil for Health*, *Ginger for Health*, *The Everything® Healthy Green Drinks Book*, and *The Everything® Green Smoothies Book*. As a competitive athlete, trainer, mom of three small children, and fitness and nutrition blogger on her own website (*www.ultimatefitmom.com*), she is well versed in the holistic approaches to keeping one's self in top performing condition.

Index